Helping Teen Moms Graduate

Helping Teen Moms Graduate

Strategies for Families, Schools, and Community Organizations

Christine M. Stroble

ROWMAN & LITTLEFIELD
Lanham • Boulder • New York • London

Published by Rowman & Littlefield
An imprint of The Rowman & Littlefield Publishing Group, Inc.
4501 Forbes Boulevard, Suite 200, Lanham, Maryland 20706
www.rowman.com

86-90 Paul Street, London EC2A 4NE, United Kingdom

Copyright © 2023 by Christine M. Stroble

All rights reserved. No part of this book may be reproduced in any form or by any electronic or mechanical means, including information storage and retrieval systems, without written permission from the publisher, except by a reviewer who may quote passages in a review.

British Library Cataloguing in Publication Information Available

Library of Congress Cataloging-in-Publication Data

Names: Stroble, Christine M., 1971– author.
Title: Helping teen moms graduate : strategies for families, schools, and community organizations / Christine M. Stroble.
Description: Lanham, Maryland : Rowman & Littlefield, [2023] | Includes bibliographical references. | Summary: "Helping Teen Moms Graduate offers practical strategies families, schools, and community organizations can employ to support pregnant and parenting students as they strive to complete their education and reduce the 50% dropout rate"—Provided by publisher.
Identifiers: LCCN 2022039821 (print) | LCCN 2022039822 (ebook) | ISBN 9781475828108 (Cloth : acid-free paper) | ISBN 9781475828115 (Paperback : acid-free paper) | ISBN 9781475828122 (epub)
Subjects: LCSH: Teenage mothers—Education (Secondary)—United States. | Teenage mothers—Services for—United States. | Community and school—United States.
Classification: LCC LB3433 .S77 2023 (print) | LCC LB3433 (ebook) | DDC 373.1826/947—dc23/eng/20220926
LC record available at https://lccn.loc.gov/2022039821
LC ebook record available at https://lccn.loc.gov/2022039822

This book is dedicated to my mother—a teen mom.

Contents

Preface	ix
Introduction	xvii
1 Don't Judge	1
2 Enforce the Law	25
3 Support from Home Matters	49
4 Support from School Matters	73
5 Support from the Community Matters	99
6 A Message to Teen Moms	119
Bibliography	131
About the Author	135

Preface

WHY I'M WRITING THIS BOOK

I have written this book to further a mission I've been on most of my life: to support teen moms. From my teen years until now, with this book, *Helping Teen Moms Graduate*, I have sought to be a source of support for teen moms.

I didn't know the term *teen mom* when I was growing up in the 1980s. The phrase used to describe a teen girl who got pregnant was "She had a baby out of wedlock," and that was a source of shame. I knew that shame, because I felt just what Brene Brown describes in her book *I Thought It Was Just Me (but It Isn't): Making the Journey from "What Will People Think?" to "I Am Enough"* on what shame is: "Shame is the intensely painful feeling or experience of believing that we are flawed and therefore unworthy of love and belonging—something we've experienced, done, or failed to do makes us unworthy of connection" (p. 29).

That something for me was, I was the product of an unwed teen mother. As far back as I can remember that's what I felt. Shame. It's one of the two most pronounced feelings that surface when I think of my childhood. No one said anything. I just felt like I wasn't good enough.

It wasn't until I was in my thirties, when I read *The Purpose Driven Life* by Rick Warren, that I started to consider that maybe I wasn't a mistake. Maybe God did have a purpose for me, even though I was born out of wedlock. I was sitting at the kitchen table, reading my morning devotional from *The Purpose Driven Life*, and it was as if God was speaking directly to me through the pages: You are not a mistake.

But I felt I was. I felt the shame, and the source was my birthright. That's where I think my mission to support teen moms comes from.

And as far back as my teen years, I have sought to be a source of support for teen moms.

Teen Years

In my teenage years, during the mid-1980s, it seemed like everyone was getting pregnant. One phrase used back then was, "It must be something in the water." As I was preparing to write this book, I was curious, wondering what the teen pregnancy rate was during the 1980s. I found the teen pregnancy rate from then, and it appears very high, but there's no way to compare it to rates now. The Centers for Disease Control and Prevention (CDC) doesn't publish teen pregnancy rates; they publish teen birth rates, and the two are very different.

The teen pregnancy rate may be one number—a high number—but the teen birth rate may be much lower. Teen girls may choose not to give birth. They may choose to terminate their teen pregnancy and that would reduce the birth rate. So, the teen pregnancy rate is different from the teen birth rate, and you cannot compare the two.

Still, to put it in some perspective, the *teenage-pregnancy rate* per 1,000 in 1988 was 197 for African Americans and 93 for whites. The latest data from the CDC reveals the *teen birth rate* per 1,000 females was 16.7 in 2019. Rates were disproportionately higher for teens of color as has historically been true. The same year, in 2019, the birth rate for Hispanic teens was 25.3 and for non-Hispanic Black teens, it was 25.8, more than two times higher than for non-Hispanic White teens (11.4). This disparity has historically been the case.

The point here is to illustrate that there were a lot of Black girls getting pregnant in the 1980s. A classmate from elementary school got pregnant in middle school. She was fourteen. A fifteen-year-old neighbor got pregnant by the older boy across the street. An older girl up the street got pregnant, and I remember she went to school until she had her baby. She went to school and had her baby the next day. I almost couldn't believe that. Other classmates got pregnant. Some chose to give birth; others chose to terminate their pregnancy.

One of my ninth-grade classmates got pregnant and so did a younger friend from church, and I empathized with them. I knew they felt shame, *and* I knew very well the roles could be reversed. With my classmate, in gym class, I hovered near her, not wanting her to feel alone. For my younger friend at church, I would keep her baby during service to give her a break.

College/Young Adult Years

During college, I offered support to friends I worked with who had been teen moms. I'd give them a ride home. Just to show my support. After college, I became an English teacher, and I continued to support teen moms. My first year of teaching, one of my ninth-grade students gravitated toward me. She was a teen mom. I encouraged and supported her. She confided in me that she had been sexually abused. That was not unusual back then, and I used to think that it was not unusual for only little Black girls, but I've learned teenage White girls are victims of sexual abuse as well.

A Support Group for Teen Moms

In my sixth year of teaching, I set out to start a support group for teen moms. I was teaching at a nontraditional high school for students who needed a flexible schedule. One reason being medical issues—for themselves or, if they were already parenting, for their child. Several pregnant and parenting students had a child with significant health challenges, and others were attending evening classes to catch up in classes they had fallen behind in.

Again, I empathized with them. When I looked at them, turning aside or clutching their jacket to hide their pregnant belly, I empathized with them. I thought about how I would feel, and I thought about how my mother must have felt. I felt they needed support to encourage each other, so I set out to form a support group.

The first thing I did was to bring in a speaker who had been a teen mom herself and who went to college and earned her master's and doctorate degree. I hoped our students would be inspired by her story.

At another meeting, I brought in literature on co-dependency and the book *The Language of Letting Go*. I had attended a CoDA (Co-Dependents Anonymous) meeting a year earlier; learning about co-dependency was the first time I understood why I was the way I was. In many cases, I think teen moms are inherently co-dependent because they are dependent on others for their very survival. In many cases, they are treated as if they don't have any rights. To survive their chaotic and often dysfunctional home environment, they develop co-dependent behaviors and have major boundaries issues. These are maladaptive coping mechanisms, but they help them survive.

In preparation for the next meeting, I began searching for material online, and I stumbled upon the *Interpersonal Violence and Adolescent Pregnancy* report, published by the Healthy Teen Network. The report revealed that there is a strong connection between abuse, violence, and teen pregnancy. That they are all intertwined. The report outlined the connection and how some teen girls become pregnant directly because of interpersonal violence; others become pregnant indirectly from conditions and circumstances associated with prior sexual or physical abuse. It explained how teen moms are in violent or abusive relationships, either before, during, or after their teen pregnancy and how children of teen moms are at a greater risk for difficulties because of the pervasiveness of violence and abuse in the mother's life.

As I read that report, I became disoriented because I was reading my life, and I couldn't figure how they knew my story. This was long before I knew what qualitative and quantitative research was. I continued to read the *Interpersonal Violence and Adolescent Pregnancy* report, and what I read later in that report was a turning point in my life. It changed everything.

The report explained that parents need to heal from their own experiences of violence in order to support the healthy emotional development of their children. That without healing, it can be challenging for parents to attach, offer consistently nurturing interactions, and respond appropriately to their children's needs and demands.

The moment I read that, I had the answer to a question that had troubled me all my life: Why do my mom and I have such a difficult relationship? And there was my answer: she had not healed from her own violent experiences, so she could not support and attend to my emotional needs. That is why we had such a difficult relationship.

From there I decided I was going to heal from all the trauma in life. I began my journey of healing, but within a year, I was in a mental health crisis and I could not work, so I wasn't at that school anymore and I couldn't continue that support group. But I never forgot about the support group for teen moms.

It took me about a year to get well enough so that I could work again. When I was well enough, I took a position in higher education as an English instructor. I enjoyed higher education, and my Dean told me if I wanted to remain in higher education, I'd have to earn my PhD. I had no interest in earning a PhD, none whatsoever, but I thought, "Okay, I can conduct research in the area of education for teen moms and their children." So, that's what I did. I enrolled in the doctoral program at The University of North Carolina at Charlotte.

Doctoral Studies on Teen Moms

In my doctoral program, I continued my efforts to support teen moms when at UNC, Charlotte. On my application for admission to the program, I specifically wrote my purpose for earning this degree was to equip me to lead a support group for teen moms.

In the four years it took me to earn my doctorate, I conducted research on improving education for teen moms. I learned about the dropout crisis among teen mothers, which I know now is more of a push out rate than dropout rate. Dropout implies pregnant and parenting students give up, but more often they are pushed out. But back then what I learned was only 50 percent earn a high school diploma and less than 2 percent earn a college degree by age thirty. I learned about the negative outcomes for children of teen moms.

When I thought about the 50 percent high dropout rate, I thought about my childhood friend from church. She had still graduated and gone off to college. I wondered, "How was she able to and so many other teen moms are not?"

I suspected the answer—she had support—but I wanted data, so I conducted a study. I interviewed female college students who had experienced a teen pregnancy in high school, and still graduated and went to college. I wanted to know, How did you do it? What helped you? My goal was to share the findings to help more teen moms graduate, thus reducing the 50 percent dropout rate. I have done that in publishing peer-reviewed works and now I've written this book, *Helping Teen Moms Graduate*.

Seven-Year Book Contract

I have had this book contract for seven years. At times I thought I'd never complete it. For several years, I struggled with a major health challenge, but the publisher would not let me abandon this project. When I was ill, they gave me space, but every few months they reached out, encouraging me to write this book.

Finally, two years ago, I was well enough and in a space where I could write this book. I am so thankful. I think it's going to make a tremendous impact and I'm so thankful I was able to complete it.

Teen Moms Anonymous

When I started writing again two years ago, I also started again with that support group for teen moms. I decided to call it Teen Moms Anonymous. Teen Moms Anonymous is a community-based support group and recovery program for teen moms who are trauma survivors. Participation is open to both teen girls ages fifteen to nineteen who are currently pregnant and parenting (with written consent from a parent or guardian) and adult women who were teen moms and are still living with unresolved trauma. Teen Moms Anonymous is open to both current teen moms and adult woman who once were. There is an advantage to having both age groups in one support group class. They can encourage each other. Our mission is to help teen moms who are trauma survivors heal from their own violent experiences so they can support the healthy emotional development of their children. This is something my mother never had the opportunity to do: heal from her trauma.

So, from my teen years until now, I have sought to be a source of support for teen moms. This is why I have written *Helping Teen Moms Graduate*.

WHY THE SUBJECT IS IMPORTANT

This subject is important because teen moms need at a minimum a high school diploma to financially provide for themselves and their child.

Without a high school diploma, their earning potential is limited. Their career options are few. With little financial means, they're unable to provide for their children. This causes a ripple effect, affecting all other areas of their lives and negatively impacting their children. To counter these negative impacts, it's important to help teen moms graduate.

This subject is also important because how we support teen moms, or do not support them, as they strive to complete their education, will determine who shows up in our preschool and elementary classrooms in five years. If we want students to come prepared and ready to learn, at the minimum, we have to support their mother and help her graduate.

WHAT I HOPE READERS WILL LEARN BY READING THE BOOK

What I hope readers will learn from reading *Helping Teen Moms Graduate* is a greater insight into the myriad challenges pregnant and parenting students face. I hope they will come away armed with specific steps they can take to help pregnant and parenting teens graduate. Steps like Don't Judge. I hope everyone will come away realizing how painful it is for pregnant and parenting students when others judge them. I hope educators will come away with a renewed commitment to fulfill their obligation to pregnant and parenting students as outlined in their mission, vision, and values. I hope educators will come away with a renewed commitment to enforce the law—Title IX as it relates to pregnant and parenting students.

I hope families will come away realizing they play a part in helping their student graduate. Schools can't do everything. I hope community partners will come away driven to continue their efforts in supporting pregnant and parenting students and in advocating for services for them, such as childcare and other support services. I hope educators, families, and community partners all come away knowing it takes a village—all of us working together to help pregnant and parenting students graduate. Together, we can reduce the 50 percent push out rate and help teen moms graduate. Let's work together and do it!

ACKNOWLEDGMENTS

No one writes a book alone. Support and encouragement from others are a necessity. I'd like to acknowledge and thank those who supported and encouraged me and were instrumental in my writing this book.

Tom Koerner with Rowman & Littlefield. Were it not for Tom's persistence and encouragement, I would not have finished this book. Over the years, Tom kept emailing, telling me he really thinks this book is needed. Thank you, Tom, for your persistence.

My mother, Wilma S. Jones. My mother was a 24-year-old Black single mom with three children in the 1970s in a place that was still very much a Jim Crow South. She was denied child support. She refused government assistance because society did, and still does today, stereotype Black single moms as welfare queens who live off the government. She didn't want that stigma attached to her, so to maintain a semblance of dignity and self-respect in a society that treated her like she was nothing, she refused government assistance. This book is for you, mom. For your sacrifice, your faithfulness, for never giving up, for never leaving us, for putting us in the church. We survived because you put us in the church. Thank you.

My son, Christian, for bringing me so much joy and laughter these last fourteen years. You make my life so much richer.

My professor, Dr. Greg Wiggan at The University of North Carolina at Charlotte. Dr. Wiggan has supported me from the time I walked into his office to inquire about the doctoral program to writing this book. He has supported me. Thank you.

The young ladies who shared their stories with me. Those who welcomed me into their homes, who met me at the library, and at Dunkin' Donuts. Thank you. Thank you for trusting me with your stories.

My family and friends who were kind enough to read this book and offer feedback, and those who have supported me and encouraged me down through the years.

Finally, I want to thank God. Thank you for being a promise keeper. Thank you for sustaining me. Thank you for all the reminders down through the years that though the vision tarry, wait for it, because it will surely come.

Introduction

Helping Teen Moms Graduate is organized into six chapters. Each chapter covers an aspect of what will help pregnant and parenting students graduate. This information is from research and case studies. The information from case studies was gathered during interviews with female college students who had all experienced a teen pregnancy and still graduated from high school on time and went to college. At the time of the interviews, graduates were either enrolled in college or had recently graduated from college.

Woven into chapters are their stories of what helped them graduate from high school. Stories of a strong female family member who wouldn't let them give up. Stories of teachers who did more than educate. They inspired, encouraged, and challenged them to not let their teen pregnancy hold them back. You will hear their stories of being part of teen parenting programs that were driven to help them graduate "by any means necessary."

Chapter 1 covers the resounding message from graduates to educators about how to help teen moms graduate: Don't Judge. You will read graduates' accounts of harsh looks, disapproval, judgments, and how those hurt them. You will read, aside from treating others as you wish to be treated, reasons not to judge. Judgment:

1. Goes against the school's vision and mission statements and core values/beliefs.
2. Creates an environment of discouragement.
3. Gets in the way of providing much needed support.
4. Doesn't consider the whole story.
5. Leads to shame, and shame is debilitating.

You will read how judgment leads to shame, and shame unravels connection—the very thing that teen moms need. You will read how the antidote to shame is empathy because empathy fuels connection. For pregnant and parenting students already feeling inadequate, feeling connected becomes increasingly important.

Chapter 2 covers Title IX and the critical importance of enforcing this federal law as it relates to pregnant and parenting students. Title IX is a federal law that prohibits federally funded educational institutions—from elementary to university level—from discriminating against students or employees based on sex. Title IX is best known for its application to female athletes, but Title IX also applies to pregnant and parenting students. It prohibits discrimination against them and protects their right to an education equal to their peers. In this chapter, you will read that while Title IX has made significant gains and progress for female athletes—opening doors and creating opportunities—this same progress does not ring true for pregnant and parenting students.

Almost fifty years after the passage of Title IX in 1972, still 50 percent of pregnant and parenting students do not earn a high school diploma. This is in large part because:

- Educational barriers push pregnant and parenting students out of school.
- Schools are in direct violation of Title IX.

Chapter 2 discusses these two factors. It also includes recommendations from the U.S. Department of Education, Office for Civil Rights (OCR), and the National Women's Law Center (NWLC) to ensure schools are enforcing the law.

Chapters 3, 4, and 5 are supportive chapters covering how support from home matters, support from school matters, and support from the community matters. It takes a village, and each chapter opens with the voices of graduates singing praises and expressing their gratitude to their families, teachers, community teen parenting programs and parenting classes, and the faith community. Graduates agree that they graduated because they had support from home, teachers, and the community.

Chapter 3 covers how family support matters. Schools alone cannot address all the challenges pregnant and parenting students face. The meaningful involvement of parents and support from home is vital because many of the challenges pregnant and parenting students face are on the home front. Challenges such as getting enough sleep and managing it all. Support from home, particularly from a strong female family role model, was top of the list of reasons for graduates' success. All pregnant and parenting students don't have support from home. In this chapter you will read why many pregnant and parenting students don't have the support from home they need. This is likely because they are caught in an intergenerational cycle of teen pregnancy. This chapter looks at viable options when their mom is not able to offer support. Options like:

- A surrogate mother must step up in place of a mom.
- Fathers must take on their responsibility.

Chapter 3 also discusses a huge undertaking that would require significant and sustainable financial support, but could change the life trajectory of a pregnant or parenting student and her child. It could literally be the catalyst for generational change. This is having a residential academy for pregnant and parenting students and their children. This residential academy would be a safe place where the pregnant and parenting student and her child could call home for a few years until she completes her education and acquires job skills. This residential academy could provide onsite, high-quality childcare and all the other services pregnant and parenting students need. This school could operate much like the Harlem Children's Zone and the Oprah Winfrey Leadership Academy for Girls.

Chapter 4 covers how support from schools—especially teachers—matters. Graduates share stories of how their teachers did more than teach; they supported, encouraged, and challenged them to not let their pregnancy stop them. In this chapter you will read about classroom strategies and best evidence-based practices teachers can apply to help pregnant and parenting students thrive in school and graduate.

1. Take a trauma-informed approach.
2. Demonstrate empathy.
3. Build resilience.

This chapter explains how pregnant and parenting students are often coming from a chaotic home environment and don't have the support they need from home. In such cases, support from their teachers matters even more. Their teacher's support might be their only source of encouragement.

Chapter 5 covers support from the community. Graduates sing praises and express their gratitude to community teen parenting programs, parenting classes, and faith-based organizations. You will read how teen parenting programs and classes were vital to students' success. These programs provided childcare—a necessary component for them to finish school. You will read how graduates found encouragement from teen parenting program leaders and how they inspired and were inspired by the other pregnant and parenting students in the program or class. You will read how faith organizations played a role in helping pregnant and parenting students graduate.

Chapter 6 is specifically written to be a powerhouse encouragement tool to inspire pregnant and parenting students. In this chapter, graduates give hope to pregnant and parenting students who are thinking of giving up. Pregnant and parenting students will also read about their rights under Title IX and what to do if they are discriminated against and their rights, under this federal law, are violated.

Terminology

You will notice different terminology used when referring to pregnant and parenting students. Terms such as *pregnant and parenting*, *teen mom*, and *unwed teenage mother*.

The terminology used in school settings and organizations that support students is *pregnant and parenting*. As such, although the title of this book is *Helping Teen Moms Graduate*, in most cases the term *pregnant and parenting* is used when referring to students. In a few cases, the terms *teen mom* or *unwed teenage mother* are used when most appropriate. All terms are, however, interchangeable.

When referring to students who shared their stories of how they graduated after experiencing a teen pregnancy, the term used to refer to these students is *graduate(s)*.

I hope the information will be helpful to you. My intent was to share what I've learned with educators, families, and community partners to help teen moms graduate. I hope this information will help you do just that.

CHAPTER 1

Don't Judge

Pregnant teens become creatively savvy figuring out ways to hide their pregnancy. Wearing oversized shirts and jackets. Turning aside or clutching their jacket to hide their pregnant belly. Lying to classmates, keeping it a secret from their parents, assuring others they are simply putting on a little weight. They take painstaking efforts to keep their secret confidential, to the point of self-denial.

Unbeknownst to them, there are long-term consequences to keeping such a secret due to fear, judgment, and scorn: Inadequate prenatal care. No Lamaze classes or a doula to walk them through the process. No home visits from a nurse.

Students take these measures in large part to avoid their greatest fear: being judged, shunned, looked down upon, and shamed. As you read this chapter, you'll hear the voice of graduates and new moms on how they were judged, and resounding messages to educators, loved ones, and other supporters on how to help pregnant and parenting students graduate: Don't Judge.

To judge someone in its simplest definition is determining a person's value, worth, or potential based on one's biases. Judgment shows up in varying ways societally. We see it when a woman clutches and pulls her purse close to her body when someone she considers questionable walks by. We see it when a person dressed casually is treated markedly different in a business from someone in professional attire.

Sadly, pregnant and parenting students see it in the grouped whispering of peers. Even more disturbing, they experience it when teachers, administrators, and others lower their expectations once their pregnancy is obvious. When someone assumes and responds from their determination of another's condition, status, wealth, education, or race/culture, judgment is at play.

"Don't be judgmental. Even if—if someone's having judgmental thoughts about you, even if they don't come outright and say it, you can still tell." You can still tell. This is part of one graduate, Xiomara's, sentiments in an illuminating truth for a wealth of teenaged, unwed mothers. They can feel the wave of judgmental thoughts hurled in their direction. Though the words may not be spoken, the doubt, rebuke and judgment are there.

Unfortunately, pregnant and parenting students even feel judged by some of their teachers positioned to wonderfully impact and transform their lives and the lives of their children. These students internalize the blow of that judgment from their teachers.

> "Don't be judgmental. Even if—if someone's having judgmental thoughts about you, even if they don't come outright and say it, you can still tell."
>
> —Xiomara, a graduate and college student

Like Xiomara, Alger could tell her teacher was judging her. She didn't say a word; however, it was clearly evident in her discriminating actions:

> She [the teacher] was definitely judging me, but she didn't say anything in particular. I could just tell by her actions. I could look at my friend's tests, and her tests [score] would be better than mine, and I'm looking at mine, and we almost had the exact same answers. I'm not saying that I wanted her to show pity on me, but I felt like my test was very similar. I would go to her about it; and she would be like, "Well, that's not negotiable, and my grades are final." She was very, very difficult for no reason. I feel it was because I was pregnant. This same teacher was trying to convince another girl that I needed to actually get an abortion.

Being judged causes pregnant and parenting students to lose confidence in themselves. It causes doubt and decreased self-worth. It leads to feelings of inadequacy and not being good enough. That was Xiomara and Alger's reality.

Xiomara experienced the air of judgment in two more stark ways for a young woman. The first from the community's idea of what the quality of education was at the alternative school she attended.

> If I wouldn't have gotten pregnant, I could have stayed at [her home school]. A lot of people look down on [the alternative school] like they think it's easier or something. But it really is not. It's the same courses. The teachers' kind of baby you there. They're with you step-by-step. It's not like a regular high school. They're with you. They're just a lot of help.

The second part of the sting from judgment came through disapproval. It was part of Xiomara's judgment story. She lived with her mother but spent a great deal of time with her father and stepmother, whom she admired. Her stepmother had an advanced degree and wanted that for Xiomara, too. However, when she became pregnant, Xiomara got support from her mother's family, but not from the one person she wanted support from more than anyone—her stepmom. Instead of support, she was met with disapproval and rejection:

> Everyone was supportive, except the one person I really wanted support from—my stepmom. Living with my mom, I was able to do whatever I wanted. When I ended up pregnant, my stepmom was more disappointed than anything. And she wanted me to consider all of my options. Especially because I'd applied for and was selected for an internship at [said] University. I think her heart was broken more than anything.

Xiomara was hurt, but she just pushed it aside and made herself believe it didn't matter.

> I was hurt because that's who's support I wanted more than anything. I just pushed it to the side and said it doesn't matter, and as long as I have myself, or my mom's support that's all that matters. I made myself believe that.

Harsh looks, disapproval, and judgments hurt students, especially pregnant and parenting students already experiencing emotional upheaval. There is no way around that truth. Quincy attests to that. She became a teen mom at age fifteen and is clear on how being judged negatively hurt her. Her driving force to healing her pain became proving wrong those she believed were standing in judgment.

> When I was pregnant, I had all kinds of people looking at me like, "Oh, she's pregnant? She's only fifteen, and she's pregnant? Oh, that's not nice. That's not cute." And I even had some elderly people looking at me. They looked at me weird, then turned their heads, and squint their eyes like, "Well, why is she pregnant?" I could tell they were judging me.
>
> My grandmother was angry with me because I was the only child and grandchild, so they expected so much from me, and to find out that I was pregnant, it was like, "Oh, oh." Like disgust. And so, it hurt me, and I was saying to myself, "I'm going to prove all of you wrong. I'm going to prove all of you wrong; because—just because I'm pregnant does not mean I have to stop living my life." It doesn't mean that I'm not going to make the good grades that I was making, or I'm not going to be successful and go to college.

Xiomara, Alger, and Quincy were not the only pregnant and parenting students who felt judged. When Diana felt judged, that fueled feeling disconnected, and she remembers feeling like an outsider. That notion of being an outcast was traumatically present during one of the most memorable high school events—the prom. The judgment she experienced changed her life overnight. The feeling that showed up for her significantly was that she didn't belong.

> I still went to prom, but I had to do another dress because the dress that I had didn't fit anymore. It was hard for me to go to prom just because everybody looked at you differently. I just felt out of place. I mean, it just hurt me to know that people you've been going to school with all your life turn their back on you as soon as you make a mistake. I was always taught you should never judge a book by its cover. And my last semester in high school was the hardest out of my twelve years of going to school.
>
> With everybody just judging me. I got treated differently instantly. Here I was being the most popular girl in school, to getting treated like trash at the end of the day. It got to the point I didn't want to go to school anymore. I wanted to just lay in the bed and cry.

Feeling hurt is the aftermath when teachers and others judge pregnant and parenting students. Judgment takes the wind out of them. It takes away their fight and causes them to focus on proving others wrong when that time and energy would be better spent completing classes. With their fight gone, the chance of spiraling into depression and hopelessness increases. Such crushing emotions could further lead to poor prenatal care, poor performance in school, and no desire to foster supportive relationships to assist in their growing family.

REASONS NOT TO JUDGE

Graduates were clear on how they felt judged and how it hurt them. They are clear on what administrators, teachers, and others can do to help pregnant and parenting students graduate: Don't Judge. Along with "treat others as you would have them treat you," there are several other reasons teachers, administrators, and others should not judge pregnant and parenting students:

1. Goes against the school's vision and mission statements and core values/beliefs
2. Creates an environment of discouragement
3. Gets in the way of providing much needed support
4. Doesn't consider the whole story
5. Leads to shame, and shame is debilitating

Goes against Mission, Vision, and Belief Statements

Judging pregnant and parenting students goes against a school's vision and mission statement, and their core values/beliefs. It goes against what the schools says about how students should be treated and creating a positive school climate.

A school's vision statement is a clear and concise statement that describes the school's long-term goals—where the school wants to be in the future. The mission statement explains how the school aims to achieve it long-term goals. What will the school do to be where it wants to be? Schools have both a vision and mission statement. Next are core values/beliefs.

A school's core values/beliefs are what the school fundamentally believes. Core beliefs dictate expected behaviors and can help people understand the difference between right and wrong.

Provided below is an example of one school district's vision, mission, and core values/beliefs. Administrators, teachers, and others in the school building must remember these commitments when interacting with pregnant and parenting students. These guiding principles apply to this student population, too.

Our Vision

We envision a district where:

- The focus is on students
- Students, staff, and stakeholders feel safe, valued, and respected
- Educational opportunities and facilities are designed to maximize student learning
- Students are provided opportunities outside of the classroom to grow and develop
- All students graduate with a career focus and a planned path to achieve it
- Parents and the community are engaged as partners in the education of our students

This is a vision statement—the school's long-term goals. The mission stated below is a declaration of how the school will achieve its long-term goals.

Our Mission Statement

> [Example school district], where children are always first, ensures the highest quality education for all children by providing a highly qualified staff, a challenging curriculum, first class facilities, and a safe and nurturing environment.

This mission statement tells how this district will achieve its long-term goals. Vision and mission statements work together. Schools also operate around guiding principles. These are the school's core values/beliefs. Core values/beliefs support the vision, shape the culture, and reflect what the school values. Below are this district's *Shared Values/Belief Statements*

Shared Values/Belief Statements
Excellence in Learning
We believe:

- All students can learn and are a part of a community of learners—students, faculty, and parents—who share the responsibility of education excellence.
- The effective use of instructional techniques and curricula will promote the independence and success of all students.
- Knowledge, skills, and understanding are assessed through a variety of progressively challenging and authentic activities and products.
- The high expectations of the community of learners encourage a flexible curriculum which incorporates technology, fine arts, and physical fitness into a broad academic framework.

Student Accountability and Responsibility
We believe:

- All students should be empowered to achieve at their highest levels.
- All students can demonstrate respect for all members of the community of learners.
- All students can take responsibility for their learning.

School Environment
We believe:

- Learning can best be accomplished in a safe, pleasant, and well-equipped environment.
- Our diversity provides opportunities to learn from the values and cultures of others.
- The community of learners is committed to a team approach.
- The community of learners values the challenge of change.

Table 1.1. Vision, Mission, and Core Values

Vision Statement	Mission Statement	Core Values
This is what your school aspires to be in its objectives and long-term goals.	This is what your school does to achieve its objectives and long-term goals.	Support the vision, shape the culture, and reflect what your school values. These are your beliefs and principles.
We envision a District where	[Said school district], where children are always first, ensures the highest quality education for all children by providing a highly qualified staff, a challenging curriculum, first class facilities, and a safe and nurturing environment.	—Excellence in Learning
—Students, staff, and stakeholders feel safe, valued, and respected.		—Student Accountability and Responsibility
		—School Environment

Realistically, casting judgment on pregnant and parenting students thwarts the vision, mission, and core values/beliefs that the school espouses: We envision a district where students, staff, and stakeholders feel safe, valued, and respected.

Judging pregnant and parenting students lessens the feeling of being safe, secure, protected, and wanted in the learning environment. Judging students also raises doubts about the genuine concern of the adults in the environment to genuinely want to lead, participate in, and promote students' success. Alger's teacher's response was indicative of this.

When administrators, teachers, and others in the school building judge pregnant and parenting students, they are not fulfilling their obligation to this student population as outlined in their vision, mission, and beliefs statements. Their actions are in stark contrast to what they say they believe and do.

Creates an Environment of Discouragement

Judging pregnant and parenting students also creates an environment of discouragement—a school climate in direct contrast to the school's vision to create a healthy campus climate that is respectful, safe, diverse, and equitable.

Graduates Xiomara, Alger, Quincy, and Renee endured this environment of discouragement. They felt the judgment, shame, and rebuke of some of their teachers and peers. Fortunately, they were able to push through feeling they were not wanted in the school building and to graduate. They were able to do this in large part because of support from home, teachers, and community programs like teen parenting programs and classes. Think of pregnant and parenting students who don't have that support.

Graduates were not the only pregnant and parenting students who faced an environment of discouragement. Students in a study and focus group conducted by the National Women's Law Center (NWLC) expressed the same sentiments (National Women's Law Center, n.d.).

With the goal to better understand what a safe and healthy school environment looks like for all girls, the NWLC collaborated with Lake Research Partners to conduct a study of girls on January 5–19, 2017. The study included an online survey of 1,003 girls ages fourteen to eighteen nationwide. The study also included six focus groups on barriers facing girls who are survivors of sexual assault and girls who are either currently pregnant or those who are parenting children.

The focus group for pregnant and parenting students, *Let Her Learn: Stopping the School Pushout for Girls Who Are Pregnant or Parenting*, yielded eleven educational barriers that hindered students' quest to complete their education (National Women's Law Center, 2017). One of the eleven identified educational barriers that pregnant and parenting students faced was an environment of discouragement: the exact school climate that goes directly against a school's vision, mission, and core values/beliefs.

Findings from *Let Her Learn: Stopping the School Pushout for Girls Who Are Pregnant and Parenting* (National Women's Law Center, 2017) reveal that girls who are pregnant or parenting often face an environment of discouragement that pushes them out of school—from some teachers' and administrators' low expectations and unwelcoming policies to outright hostility, discrimination, and direct and indirect pressure to leave school.

- According to the Let Her Learn Survey, girls who are pregnant or parenting (61 percent) were less likely than girls overall (81 percent) to say that they had someone at their school who cared about them and wanted them to succeed.

In fact, many of the girls in the Let Her Learn Focus Groups (National Women's Law Center, 2017) described a shift in how their teachers and peers perceived them once their pregnancy was known. Diane spoke to this. They felt that teachers and administrators wrote them off and that the stigma of being a "teen parent" made it harder to go to school.

Even well-meaning teachers and administrators may encourage pregnant and parenting girls to take less rigorous courses, believing that it will be too hard for a young parent to succeed in school while raising a child. One girl in the Let Her Learn Focus Groups (National Women's Law Center, 2017) felt that neither her teachers nor other students respected her because she was pregnant. Another student felt that the discrimination she faced because of her pregnancy made it harder for her to succeed in school.

These experiences are consistent with those of other pregnant or parenting girls who have been shamed and discriminated against by teachers and administrators. For example, pregnant girls have been barred from displaying their pregnant bellies in school yearbooks. In another case, a band leader refused to allow a pregnant girl to participate in a special concert because she would give the school and the band a "bad image."

This type of discouragement and discrimination makes students feel unwelcome at school. Not surprisingly, the Let Her Learn Survey (National Women's Law Center, 2017) shows that many girls who are pregnant or parenting report that other students, teachers, their family members, or principals do not want them at their schools.

Again, this is in direct opposition to why the school even exists. Regardless of educators' moral beliefs and how their views contrast with being a teen pregnant, they must set aside their beliefs because, when they don't—when they judge pregnant and parenting students—they are part of the problem. Their actions are pushing girls out of school. This does not support helping pregnant and parenting students graduate.

Let Her Learn (National Women's Law Center, 2017) also discovered that girls who are pregnant or parenting can also face both direct and indirect pressures to leave school. One charter school in Louisi-

Table 1.2. Percentage of Girls Reporting That Specific Groups of People Did Not Want Them at School

	Pregnant and Parenting Girls
Other Students	51%
Teachers	38%
Family members	26%
Their parents or guardians	25%
Principals	31%
The counselors	21%
Their mentors	20%

Source: National Women's Law Center, Let Her Learn Survey, conducted by Lake Research Partners (2017).

ana, for example, required pregnant girls to switch to another school or begin a home school program. This practice only ended when the American Civil Liberties Union filed a formal discrimination complaint, and the Louisiana Department of Education forced the school to stop pushing pregnant girls out of school. In another case, a student at a public high school in Detroit who had dropped out when she became pregnant at seventeen was denied the ability to reenroll a year later, with the school claiming that they would not be able to keep her safe.

The study also found that girls who are pregnant or parenting may also come under increased scrutiny by educators and be held to an unreasonable standard. Counselors and teachers sometimes tell student mothers that they "can't make any mistakes" and must be on their "best behavior." In the Let Her Learn Focus Groups, one girl explained, "I'm the only person pregnant in my whole school so like all eyes be on me." These pressures combined with low expectations can have a tremendous negative effect on students.

Gets in the Way of Providing Much Needed Support

Judging pregnant and parenting students also gets in the way of providing this student population with the support they need, thus creating another educational barrier that pushes girls out of school.

Lack of support was one of the educational barriers identified by students in the Let Her Learn Survey. Lack of support can make it harder for pregnant or parenting students to succeed in school.

- In the Let Her Learn Survey, more than one in four girls who are pregnant or parenting (26 percent) said that they get little or no counseling or help about their futures.

This lack of support contrasts starkly with what the girls in the Let Her Learn Focus Groups said they need to succeed in school: counselors, teachers with whom they could talk, and mentors. The girls in the focus groups also said that having help and a solid support system would allow them to achieve their dreams and goals.

Again, these two educational barriers—an environment of discouragement and lack of support—go against the school's obligation to this student population. When administrators, teachers, and others in the building cast judgment on pregnant and parenting students, they create an environment of discouragement and do not provide this student population the support they need. When schools do this, they are not leading pregnant and parenting students in the direction to graduate. Just the opposite. They are pushing girls out and contributing to the 50 percent push out rate for pregnant and parenting students.

Does Not Consider the Whole Story

When teachers, administrators, and others judge pregnant and parenting students, they are not considering the whole story. They're basing their judgment only on what they see, and assume the pregnant teen was just reckless to have unprotected sex and caused her own situation. They blame her, often commenting that the student just "messed up her life." But when administrators, teachers, and others hear the whole story, they will reconsider casting judgment on pregnant and parenting students.

Each pregnant and parenting teen has her own individual story, but pregnant and parenting students collectively have a story of violence and abuse. The *Interpersonal Violence and Adolescent Pregnancy* report outlines this history of violence and abuse, explaining how violence, abuse, and teen pregnancy are closely related (Leiderman & Almo, 2001). They are intertwined. Highlights from that report include:

- Many young women (as many as two-thirds) who become pregnant as adolescents were sexually and/or physically abused at

some point in their lives—either as children, in their current relationships, or both.
- A substantial number (no fewer than one-fourth and as many as 50 to 80 percent) of adolescent mothers are in violent, abusive, or coercive relationships just before, during, and after their pregnancy.
- Younger teen girls are even more likely to be victims of interpersonal violence than older teens. For example, one study found that younger teen girls are especially vulnerable to coercive and non-consensual sex. Involuntary sexual activity was found in 74 percent of sexually active girls younger than 14 and 60 percent of those younger than fifteen.
- The report notes that it is important to remember that the actual prevalence of interpersonal violence in the lives of teen girls may be higher than this data indicates. This is because victims, partners, and families often do not disclose violence or abuse in their lives, so it is frequently underreported.

> Many young women (as many as two-thirds) who become pregnant as adolescents were sexually and/or physically abused at some point in their lives—either as children, in their current relationships, or both.
>
> —*Interpersonal Violence and Adolescent Pregnancy*
> The Healthy Teen Network

The report *Interpersonal Violence and Adolescent Pregnancy* (Leiderman & Almo, 2001) continues to tell the story of how violence and abuse are linked, directly or indirectly:

- Some teens become pregnant directly because of interpersonal violence, through incest, sexual abuse, or through violence that includes birth control sabotage.
- Others become pregnant indirectly through correlating circumstances or conditions associated with prior sexual or physical abuse.
- For example, abused children may remain in an unsafe situation where they are likely to be exposed to additional sexual advances.

- They may experience emotional and psychological damage that makes them especially vulnerable to coercive and violent partners when they leave home.
- As adolescents, they may be depressed and self-medicate with drugs or alcohol.
- All these circumstances and conditions put them at high risk of teen pregnancy, compared to adolescents who were not abused as children.

So, for many pregnant and parenting students, contributing factors like violence and abuse led directly or indirectly to their teen pregnancy. She didn't become a teen mom necessarily by choice. Motherhood was thrust upon her. Yet she is judged and shamed, and others assume she became pregnant because she was irresponsible, and she is to blame for her situation. She made her bed hard, so she must lie in it. But abuse and violence often contributed to her having a teen pregnancy.

Instead of judging the pregnant and parenting student in your school or sitting in your classroom, consider her as an infant. She was born innocent. Then consider her backstory. Ask yourself what happened to her growing up that caused her current state. That will cause educators and others to hit *pause* on judging her very quickly.

> A substantial number (no fewer than one-fourth and as many as 50 to 80 percent) of adolescent mothers are in violent, abusive, or coercive relationships just before, during, and after their pregnancy.
>
> —*Interpersonal Violence and Adolescent Pregnancy*
> The Healthy Teen Network

Adverse Childhood Experiences

You've already read about the collective history of violence and abuse prevalent in the lives of pregnant and parenting students. These events are classified as adverse childhood experiences (ACEs). ACEs are events that occur in the first eighteen years of your life and are divided into three major categories with subcategories. They include:

- Abuse—emotional, physical, sexual
- Neglect—emotional, physical
- Household challenges
    - Mother treated violently
    - Substance abuse in the household
    - Mental illness in the household
    - Parental separation or divorce
    - Incarcerated household member

According to the Centers for Disease and Control and Prevention (CDC), experiencing these ACEs can have a lasting effect on many areas of a person's life (CDC, 2022):

> ACEs can have lasting, negative effects on health, well-being, as well as life opportunities such as education and job potential. These experiences can increase the risks of injury, sexually transmitted infections, maternal and child health problems (including teen pregnancy, pregnancy complications, and fetal death), involvement in sex trafficking, and a wide range of chronic diseases and leading causes of death such as cancer, diabetes, heart disease, and suicide.

The CDC (2022) further notes that:

> ACEs and associated social determinants of health, such as living in under-resourced or racially segregated neighborhoods, frequently moving, and experiencing food insecurity, can cause toxic stress (extended or prolonged stress). Toxic stress from ACEs can negatively affect children's brain development, immune systems, and stress-response systems. These changes can affect children's attention, decision-making, and learning.

ACEs and Rates of Depression

Considering the prevalence of ACEs in the lives of pregnant and parenting students, it's understandable that rates of depression would be high for this student population. A journal article, "Addressing the Mental Health Needs of Pregnant and Parenting Adolescents," published in *Pediatrics*, provides alarming information concerning depression among pregnant and parenting students (Hodgkinson et al., 2014):

A number of studies suggest that adolescent mothers experience significantly higher rates of depression, both prenatally and postpartum, than adult mothers and their nonpregnant peers. Among adolescent mothers, rates of depression are estimated to be between 16% and 44%. In contrast, the lifetime prevalence of major depression among nonpregnant adolescents and adult women is between 5% and 20%. Depression symptoms among young mothers are also more likely to persist well after the birth of their child. Although there are few prospective, longitudinal studies on the long-term mental health outcomes of adolescent mothers, one study of African American adult women who became mothers during adolescence found a twofold increase in depression 20 years after the birth of their first child.

Consistent with this data on the prevalence of depression among pregnant and parenting students, data from *Let Her Learn: Stopping School Pushout for Girls Who Are Pregnant or Parenting* (National Women's Law Center, 2017) revealed yet another educational barrier pregnant and parenting students face that push them out of school. In addition to the environment of discouragement and lack of support already mentioned, pregnant and parenting students experience *negative feelings*.

Let Her Learn found that many girls who are pregnant or parenting experience symptoms of depression and posttraumatic stress disorder.

Table 1.3. Girls Reporting Negative Feelings

Felt bad about themselves or were a failure or let everyone down	74%
Felt down or depressed or hopeless	79%
Had repeated disturbing memories, thoughts, or images of a stressful experience from the past	82%
Felt afraid as if something awful might happen	72%
Felt angry about how they were treated	82%
Had thoughts that they would be better off dead or hurting themselves	61%

Source: National Women's Law Center, Let Her Learn Survey, conducted by Lake Research Partners (2017). Includes girls who say they experienced the feeling more often than not or occasionally.

Similarly, parenting students in the *Let Her Learn* study (National Women's Law Center, 2017) identified stress and anxiety as one of their biggest concerns.

- In the Let Her Learn Survey, nearly nine in ten girls who were pregnant or parenting (89 percent) said that providing a crisis counselor would help to make schools better for girls.

Considering the impact of ACEs on mental health that a large percentage of pregnant and parenting students have experienced, this is all the more reason not to judge them. They have had enough of that. Instead of judging them, pregnant and parenting students need understanding and support to help them graduate.

Special Consideration—Children of Teen Mothers

A special note needs to be considered regarding children of pregnant and parenting students. *Interpersonal Violence and Adolescent Pregnancy* (Leiderman & Almo, 2001) noted that children of adolescents are at a high risk for difficulties stemming from the pervasiveness of violence and abuse in their parents' lives. This is important to note because some of the pregnant or parenting students in your school or sitting in your classroom are the product of a teen mom.

> Children of adolescents are at high risk for difficulties stemming from the pervasiveness of violence and abuse in their parents' lives. They are at direct risk if they continue to be raised in abusive or violent settings or if the parents continue to form unhealthy partnerships and/or have few safe living alternatives (a serious problem for adolescents with children). Their parents' ability to provide for them can be compromised by education or employment sabotage (where a controlling partner limits a parent's ability to go to school, look for work or keep a job), and/or by substance abuse, anxiety, depression, and other symptoms of trauma, violence, and abuse. (By way of illustration, 92% of poor, homeless women are previous or current victims of domestic abuse, according to Ellen Bassuk, Director of the Better Homes Fund.)

Finally, the report (Leiderman & Almo, 2001) concludes:

> There is increasing evidence that parents need to heal from their own violent experiences in order to support the healthy emotional development of their children. Without healing, it can be challenging for parents

to attach, offer consistently nurturing interactions and respond appropriately to their children's needs and demands.

In terms of risk, it is tough to be a child of an abuse survivor, even an aware and recovering one. It is not easy to be the child of an adolescent who is likely to be struggling to complete his or her own education, earn an income, and manage a family. Evidence suggests that it may be especially difficult to be both.

If the student sitting in your classroom is the product of a teen parent, and her mother has not healed from her own violent experiences, that will impact the mother's ability to effectively parent and attend to her daughter's emotional needs, thus putting her daughter at risk for ACEs and teen pregnancy.

Considering all the adverse childhood experiences pregnant and parenting students have endured, and the impact of that trauma on their mental health, the last thing these students need is administrators, teachers, and others judging them. That pushes them out of school and contributes to the 50 percent push out rate for pregnant and parenting students.

Judgment Leads to Shame

Judging students leads to shame, and shame is debilitating. Shame causes you to withdraw and retreat. The sting of shames causes you feel you are not good enough. Judgment and shame go hand-in-hand. Think of times you have felt judged; shame likely raised its head as well. Shame and vulnerability researcher and author Brene Brown defines shame as:

> the intensely painful feeling or experience of believing that we are flawed and therefore unworthy of love and belonging—something we've experienced, done, or failed to do makes us unworthy of connection. (Taylor, 2016)

Brown further notes that although

> shame feels isolating, *everyone experiences it* (with the exception of severe psychopaths). While no one *wants* to share their insecurities, talking

about shame is the only way to diminish its power because, once you know that you're not alone, shame loses its leverage.

Brown contends that talking about shame, takes away its power: "If we cultivate enough awareness about shame, to name it and speak to it, we've basically cut it off at the knees. It loses its power over us." It can no longer hold pregnant and parenting students hostage.

Considering what shame needs to thrive—secrecy, silence, and judgment—it makes sense that pregnant and parenting students are riddled with feelings of shame. Shame thrives as they try to hide their pregnancy. Shame increases as they face judgment from peers and adults in the school. Shame explodes when disappointment storms upon them in their families.

With shame partnered with judgment, pregnant and parenting students facing parenthood find a new struggle to overcome. Imagine a teenage girl walking down a school hallway; she sees the stares and hears the snickering and whispering of peers. As she continues to her next class, she notices one of her teachers.

That teacher is looking at her in a questionable manner. She always respected this teacher and felt the teacher liked her. That was before her pregnant belly, she thinks, became so prominent. She feels judged on her walk through a school she's attended for a couple of years. That judgment brings along shame. That shame makes her question her worthiness as a student and as a potential graduate.

With shame overwhelming her, she pays less attention in class and struggles to complete assignments. She wonders why she is no longer invited to study groups or after-school discussions. Though it may not be intentional, she believes it is, and shame increases. So judgment brings increasing emotional, mental, and intellectual downturns in the world of the teen-mom-in-waiting. This increase is piled onto a young student who is already struggling with anxiety and depression, and maybe even addiction.

Teachers, administrators, and others can help pregnant and parenting students come from underneath their shame. They must encourage and create an environment where shame and judgment are not in the room. Doing so increases graduation success rates.

Connection Is Why We Are Here

Everyone wants to feel connected. In her TED Talk, "The Power of Vulnerability," Brown explains that *connection is why we are all here* (Brown, 2010):

> It's [connection] what gives purpose and meaning to our lives. This is what it's all about. It doesn't matter whether you talk to people who work in social justice, mental health and abuse and neglect, what we know is that connection, the ability to feel connected, is—neurobiologically that's how we're wired—it's why we're here.

Pregnant and parenting students need to feel a sense of connection even more. They need to feel they belong in the school and classrooms but judgment leads to shame, and shame "unravels connection."

Shame Unravels Connection

Brown explains that the problem with shame is it unravels connection—the very thing we all need.

- Shame can be understood as the fear of disconnection; the fear that there is something about me that makes others consider me unworthy of connection.
- Shame is universal. We all have it. The only people who don't experience shame have no capacity for human empathy or connection.
- No one wants to talk about shame, and the less you talk about it, the more you have it.
- Shame is expressed in the feeling of "I'm not _____ enough" (good enough, thin enough, rich enough, beautiful enough, smart enough, promoted enough, etc.).

The less you talk about shame, the more you have it. The more you have it, the more it forces you to flee from connection. Shame is what Xiomara, Alger, Quincy, and Diane all felt. They felt that they didn't belong and were not wanted. Thankfully, they had support to overcome not feeling wanted in the school building and went on to graduate, but

> The unwed pregnant teen void of connection is also void of needed support, guidance, and encouragement. When you look at the changing narrative of an expectant teen mother, the absence of connection can be devastating.

it wasn't easy. But they did it because they were connected to a strong female at home, to their teachers and to other pregnant and parenting students in their teen parenting programs and classes.

For students who are pregnant and parenting and already feeling inadequate, feeling connected becomes increasingly important. When they feel connected, they feel included and a part of the group, and they are then more likely to overcome feelings of being judged and shamed. They are more likely to graduate.

Empathy Fuels Connection

Brown contends that empathy is the antidote or remedy to shame. Empathy fuels connection and in her TED Talk, *Listening to Shame*, Brown explains shame and why empathy is the antidote:

> Shame is an epidemic in our culture. And to get out from underneath it, to find our way back to each other, we have to understand how it affects us and how it affects the way we're parenting, the way we're working, the way we're looking at each other. . . .
>
> If we're going to find our way back to each other, we have to understand and know empathy, because empathy's the antidote to shame. If you put shame in a Petri dish, it needs three things to grow exponentially: secrecy, silence, and judgment. If you put the same amount of shame in a Petri dish and douse it with empathy, it can't survive. The two most powerful words when we're in struggle: me too. (Brown, 2012)

Empathy fuels connection. It is the ability to emotionally connect with what other person feels, see things from their point of view, and imagine yourself in their place. This is what pregnant and parenting students need from administrators, teachers, and others.

"The two most powerful words when we're in struggle: me too."

—Brene Brown, Shame and Vulnerability Researcher

Everyone Can Demonstrate Empathy

Administrators, teachers, and others can all demonstrate empathy to pregnant and parenting students. Everyone can put themselves in the shoes of a pregnant or parenting student and be aware of and sensitive to her feelings. Demonstrating empathy toward her can be a balm for the shame she is feeling. It can help her remain in school. There are a number of ways to demonstrate empathy. Below are some strategies Charter for Compassion offers (Charter for Compassion, n.d.).

Listen Listening is one of the most important ways you can demonstrate empathy, and this means truly listening—without interrupting. When you listen to someone, you aren't distracted by what is going on around you—you're really taking in what the other person is saying. True listening means being present.

You can show a pregnant or parenting student you are listening to her by facing her and looking her in the eye. Demonstrate in your body language that you are paying attention and care about what she has to say. Try to hear what she is not saying.

When you listen to someone, you build a connection. The comfort level increases, and the person in distress might pour his or her heart out. This is then the ideal opportunity to learn what she needs and how you can better support her.

Withhold Judgment From graduates' experiences, you have read what it feels like to be judged. You have read that judgment leads to shame and that shame unravels connection—the very thing a pregnant and parenting student desperately needs. Yet empathy fuels connection. So, instead of judging a pregnant or parenting student, demonstrate empathy. Listen to her. Talk to her. Make the connection. That will keep you out of judgment.

Open Up Just listening to someone isn't going to build a bridge between the two of you. Opening up emotionally—sharing your own vulnerabilities—will make that emotional connection with another person. Pregnant and parenting students need this emotional connection. They need to know they are not alone.

You don't have to tell your life story, but think of a time when you felt judged or shamed. Or misunderstood. Think of how you felt when you were judged. Then, be to that pregnant or parenting student what you needed someone to be to you. Show her the empathy you needed someone to show you.

Offer Physical Affection Offering affection could be: you give her a hug, put an arm around her shoulder, a hand on her arm. (Male counterparts may not want to do this). This type of warm embrace shows that your attention is focused on her, and it creates a connection between the two of you—what pregnant and parenting students need.

Offer Help Offering help shows that you see what the pregnant or parenting student is going through, and you want to make life easier. An example is offering her this book and letting her read the experiences of her peers and how they graduated. That will inspire her. It could mean offering to help her keep up in class. Or for a family member, it could mean taking care of her little one, so she can get adequate sleep. It could mean the administrator letting her know he/she will work with her to excuse additional absences if she just needs time to rest (if this is possible). Offering help is a great act of empathy because it shows that you're willing to take time out of your schedule to do something for her without asking anything in return.

Empathy is what pregnant and parenting students need. Empathy is the ability to emotionally connect with what the other person feels, see things from their point of view, and imagine yourself in their place. This is what pregnant and parenting students need from administrators, teachers, and others. They need you to demonstrate empathy and doing so will help pregnant and parenting students graduate.

"The struggle of my life created empathy—I could relate to pain, being abandoned, having people not love me."

—Oprah Winfrey

Don't Judge

In this chapter, graduates were clear on the advice they would give administrators, teachers, and others on how to help pregnant and parenting students graduate: Don't Judge. Quincy, Alger, Xiomara, and Diane shared their stories of what it felt like when others judged them. This chapter outlined reasons not to judge pregnant and parenting students. Beyond treating others as you wish to be treated, judging:

1. Goes against the school's vision and mission statements and core values/beliefs
2. Creates an environment of discouragement
3. Gets in the way of providing much-needed support
4. Doesn't consider the whole story
5. Leads to shame, which unravels connection

Discussed in this chapter was the antidote to shame: empathy. Empathy is the ability to emotionally connect with what the other person feels, see things from their point of view, and imagine yourself in their place. This is what pregnant and parenting students need from administrators, teachers, and others to help them graduate: Demonstrate empathy. Make a concerted effort to listen to them, open up—share with them your vulnerabilities—and offer help. Doing so is a small part everyone can play in helping pregnant and parenting students graduate.

CHAPTER 2

Enforce the Law

The television sitcom *Reba*, which premiered in the fall of 2001, endeared and enraged many families with one of its main storylines. That storyline revolved around the main character's pregnant teenage daughter, Cheyenne. Cheyenne represented the average popular teenage girl—cheerleader, loving and supportive parents, living in suburbia, dating the star school football player. And sexually active without her parent's knowledge.

When the character's pregnancy was fully evident, the high school principal asked her to consider enrolling in a school for pregnant teenagers. The principal believed Cheyenne's pregnancy set a negative precedent and example in the public high school she oversaw. That school administrator's attitude mirrored a once-popular mantra: You show, you go.

To prevent such discrimination and to protect a pregnant or parenting student's right to an education, Congress passed Title IX of the Educational Amendment Acts of 1972 (Title IX). Title IX prohibits federally funded educational institutions from discriminating against students or employees based on sex—including pregnancy, parenting, and all related conditions. In this chapter, you will read more about pregnant and parenting students' protection under Title IX and the urgent and critical importance of enforcing this federal law to help pregnant and parenting students graduate.

Title IX, a federal law that prohibits discrimination based on sex in educational institutions, begins with:

> No person in the United States shall, on the basis of sex, be excluded from participation in, be denied the benefits of, or be subjected to discrimination under any education program or activity receiving Federal financial assistance. (This Day in History, 1972)

As a result of Title IX, any school that receives any federal money from the elementary to university level—nearly all schools—must provide fair and equal treatment of the sexes in all areas, including athletics.

Title IX is best known for creating opportunities for female athletes.[1] Before Title IX, few opportunities existed for female athletes. The National Collegiate Athletic Association (NCAA), which was created in 1906 to format and enforce rules in men's football but had become the ruling body of college athletics, offered no athletic scholarships for women and held no championships for women's teams. Furthermore, facilities, supplies, and funding were lacking. As a result, in 1972 there were just 30,000 women participating in NCAA sports, as opposed to 170,000 men (This Day in History, 1972).

Title IX was designed to correct those imbalances. Although it did not require that women's athletics receive the same amount of money as men's athletics, it was designed to enforce equal access and quality. Women's and men's programs were required to devote the same resources to locker rooms, medical treatment, training, coaching, practice times, travel and per diem allowances, equipment, practice facilities, tutoring, and recruitment. Scholarship money was to be budgeted on a commensurate basis, so that if 40 percent of a school's athletic scholarships were awarded to men, 40 percent of the scholarship budget was also earmarked for women.

Since the enactment of Title IX, women's participation in sports has grown exponentially. In high schools, the number of girl athletes has increased from just 295,000 in 1972 to more than 2.6 million. In colleges, the number has grown from 30,000 to more than 150,000. Title IX has indeed opened the door and created significant opportunities for female athletes.

TITLE IX AND PREGNANT OR PARENTING STUDENTS

Title IX doesn't just apply to female athletes; it was also designed to protect the rights of female students who are pregnant or parenting. Title IX prohibits discrimination on the basis of sex—including pregnancy, parenting, and all related conditions—in education and in programs and activities that receive federal funding. All students who might be, are, or have been pregnant have a right to the same access to school programs and educational opportunities that other students have. This applies up through the university level.

Before Title IX, like the fictional TV character Cheyenne, pregnant and parenting students were being denied the right to an education. They were being dismissed or expelled. Title.info, whose mission is to explain the regulation and continuing restrictive amendments with easy understanding declares,

> What a waste of potential! If a teenager became pregnant, she usually lost her chance to get an education. Most schools expelled pregnant students and wouldn't let them return to school if they chose to continue the pregnancy. (*10 Key Areas of Title IX, Education for Pregnant and Parenting Students*, n.d.)

Title IX made such discrimination against pregnant and parenting students illegal. According to TitleIX.info, under Title IX, pregnant and parenting students' rights to an education is protected:

> Title IX protects pregnant teenagers, their children, and their futures. Under Title IX, schools are not allowed to treat pregnant or parenting students like second-class citizens. The law recognizes how important it is for all young people to have access to education, not just for their future economic independence and self-sufficiency, but also for the health and development of their children. Schools can have separate programs for pregnant students, but enrollment in these programs must be voluntary, and they must be of comparable quality to the other programs the school offers. (*10 Key Areas of Title IX, Education for Pregnant and Parenting Students*, n.d.)

Under this federal law, a pregnant or parenting student can no longer be asked to leave school or encouraged to attend an alternative school—the way Cheyenne's principal suggested she go to an alternative school. Under Title IX, a pregnant or parenting student can no longer be expelled or dismissed from school. Title IX mandates:

- A school must provide equal access to school and extracurricular activities for students who are pregnant, who have been pregnant, or who have a child, and special services provided for temporarily disabled students must be provided for pregnant students as well.

- Separate programs or schools for pregnant and parenting students must be completely voluntary and must offer opportunities equal to those offered for non-pregnant students.
- Absences due to pregnancy or childbirth must be excused for as long as is deemed medically necessary by the student's doctor.
- A doctor's note can be required for pregnant students to participate in activities only if the school requires a doctor's note from all students who have conditions that require medical care.

An example of the success of Title IX is found with one graduate, Kelly. Kelly became pregnant at fifteen, while a cheerleader in school. Because her pregnancy was considered high risk, she stopped cheering soon after learning she was with child. A year after her daughter's birth, with gossip, advice, and naysayers swirling around her, she joined the cheerleading squad again.

> If I couldn't cheer and I was on the team and I had a baby, they'd probably be looking at me like, "Hmm . . ." Ain't no telling. There was probably some talk going around, like, "She just had a baby a year ago." But I was doing my thing. I was not going to let it [being a teen mom] stop me.

While cheer coaches and others may have been concerned about Kelly returning to the squad, thanks to Title IX, her decision to try out and eventually earn a spot was protected.

Still High Push Out Rate

Title IX has created significant gains for female athletes and is credited with decreasing the dropout rate of girls from high school and increasing the number of women who pursue higher education and complete college degrees. However, *this progress does not ring true for pregnant and parenting students*.

Almost fifty years after the passage of Title IX in 1972, there is still a 50 percent push out rate for pregnant and parenting students. This crisis was addressed in the 2018 article "Fewer Teen Moms but Still a Dropout Puzzle for Schools" in *U.S. News and World Report* (The Hechinger Report, 2018):

With U.S. high school graduation rates surpassing 84 percent and hitting *record highs*, year after year, it's easy to forget that there are still pockets of people for whom graduating from high school is still a big challenge. One is *special-needs students. Another is pregnant and parenting students.*

It's particularly tempting to overlook this latter group because of the rapid decline in *teen pregnancies* over the last 25 years. The teen birth rate plunged more than 60 percent from 1991 to 2014, the most recent year of data. But it is hardly a problem solved. A quarter-million teenage girls, ages 15 to 19, gave birth to babies in 2014. (The Hechinger Report, 2018)

An article in *U.S. News & World Report* (The Hechinger Report, 2018) notes, "What happens to the education of these young women?" Many, as the article notes, do not earn a high school diploma:

Only 53 percent of women in their 20s who first became mothers when they were teenagers completed a traditional high school degree, according to a January 2018 report released by the nonprofit research organization Child Trends. Another 17 percent earned their high-school equivalency diploma by passing the GED test. By contrast, 90 percent of women who did not give birth as teens obtained a traditional high school diploma. (The Hechinger Report, 2018)

Jennifer Manlove, a sociologist at Child Trends who co-authored the report, notes that prevention efforts should continue, but attention must also focus on intervention:

We should maintain a focus on preventing teen births, but we also need to help improve the educational attainment of women once they become teen parents. . . . Improving outcomes for young mothers can often improve outcomes for their children. (The Hechinger Report, 2018)

The rings true also according to the latest data from the Centers for Disease and Control (CDC; *Reproductive Health: Teen Pregnancy*, 2021). According to the CDC, the number of teen girls giving birth is still significant. There was a total of 158,043 live births born to women aged 15 to 19 years, and only 50 percent of those young mothers will graduate and earn a high school diploma (*Reproductive Health: Teen Pregnancy*, 2021). The CDC reports:

> Only about 50% of teen mothers receive a high school diploma by 22 years of age, whereas approximately 90% of women who do not give birth during adolescence graduate from high school. (*Reproductive Health: Teen Pregnancy*, 2021)

These numbers exist despite protection from discrimination in educational institutions.

Impact of Pushing Students Out

There is a significant detriment to pregnant and parenting students not earning a high school diploma. According to the U.S. Bureau of Labor Statistics (*TED: The Economics Daily*, 2019), economic and career prospects for pregnant and parenting students who do not complete high school are limited. Those without a high school diploma earn considerably less than those with an advanced degree.

> In the third quarter of 2019, full-time workers aged 25 and older had median weekly earnings of $975. Those without a high school diploma had median weekly earnings of $606, compared with $749 for high school graduates (no college), and $874 for workers with some college or an associate degree. Workers with a bachelor's degree (and no additional degree) had median weekly earnings of $1,281. Workers with an advanced degree (master's, professional, and doctoral degrees) had median weekly earnings of $1,559 in the third quarter of 2019. (*TED: The Economics Daily*, 2019)

When you think of a parenting teen who is pushed out of high school, and the limited earning potential to provide for herself and her child, this is even more reason teachers, administrators, and others must stop the school push out of pregnant and parenting students and make every effort to help pregnant and parenting students graduate.

Median weekly earnings $600 for high school dropouts, $1,559 for advanced degree holders.

—U.S. Bureau of Labor Statistics

Why Has Title IX Not Decreased the Push Out Rate for Pregnant and Parenting Students?

Many factors contribute to why Title IX has not decreased the high school push out rate for pregnant and parenting students. Two factors will be discussed here:

1. Educational barriers that push pregnant and parenting students out of school
2. Blatant violations of Title IX, which prohibits discrimination against pregnant and parenting students

These two factors are problematic because, as seen with graduates and other pregnant and parenting students, becoming a mom caused them to take school more seriously. The problem is these educational barriers and blatant violations of Title IX are negatively impacting a student who is really committed to getting her education.

Renewed Interest in School

Often, for many pregnant and parenting students, becoming a mom renews her quest for an education. She is no longer living and striving just for herself, but for her child. This amazing revelation fosters an increase in hope and future achievement.

Even when pregnant and parenting students didn't take school that seriously prior to their pregnancy, becoming a mom rearranged their priorities and renewed their interest in getting an education. It made them take school more seriously because it wasn't just them living for themselves now; it was them living for their child. This was the case for Quincy, Renee, and Xiomara.

Quincy, who was fifteen when she became pregnant, admits there was a new sense of needing to accomplish more.

> And before then, it was just high school. I was just—I actually wasn't a wild child. That's why I was kind of surprised that I was pregnant because I wasn't a party party all the time. Of course, I went out. I was in high school. It was my first year of high school, so of course I went out, but—I really don't know. But it wasn't bad. Me having my child was—it made me look forward to doing things even though I had my outside issues. It made me want to be successful because now, it wasn't just me living my life for me. It was me living my life for me and my child.

The same recommitment to getting her education rang true for Renee. When she was asked about situations and people who helped her graduate, she responded that her motivation was her daughter:

> My daughter. She helped me make it because she helps me push myself. I look at her, and I'll be like, "I want something better for her." And I also want her to know when she got older, she would be like, "Well my momma did it all and she had me even at a young age."

Same for Xiomara who shared her frustration, but she refused to drop out. She wanted more for her daughter.

> I look back now, and I look at how things were after [my daughter] actually got here, and I don't know how I did it. I really don't know how I did it. I totally understand why people drop out when they have a child.

> Like, I wanted to so many times. I would stop and be like, "Gosh, this is so tiring. I'm sleepy. I'm tired. I just want a day where I don't have to do anything." Or "It would be so much easier if I just had to take care of [my daughter] and didn't have to worry about school." I came close so many times, but luckily, I got pregnant towards the end of my eleventh-grade year, and it's like it would be foolish for me to drop out when I only have a few more months left.

But in those moments when she was so frustrated that she wanted to drop out, her daughter motivated her.

Just looking at [my daughter] and knowing—like, I have so many different types of people in my family, and some of those people—I look at them and I'm like—not that I don't love them, but it's like I'm not going to be like that. I'm not going to live like that. I want more. Like, I want better for my child.

Quincy, Renee, and Xiomara had a renewed interest in getting their education and graduating because they were not just living for themselves. They now had a child to take care of and they wanted more for their child. Thankfully, because their right to an education was protected under Title IX, they could remain in school and not be expelled or dismissed—which is what happened to pregnant and parenting students before Title IX.

Consistent with Quincy's, Renee's, and Xiomara's renewed interest in getting their education, this renewed desire rang true for participants in the study *Let Her Learn: Stopping School Pushout for Girls Who Are Pregnant or Parenting*. The National Women's Law Center (NWLC) notes:

> Becoming pregnant or having a child should not be the end of anyone's education. In fact, becoming a parent can be a powerful motivator that encourages young women to focus on their and their children's futures. Studies have found that student mothers who had previously disengaged from school can find new reasons to return after the birth of a child. (National Women's Law Center, 2017)

Yet despite pregnant and parenting students' renewed interest in school and protection against discrimination under Title IX, students are still being pushed out of school. The National Women's Law Center notes:

> Despite the increased motivation of many young parents to succeed in school and the protection against discrimination provided by Title IX of the Education Amendments of 1972 ("Title IX"), many girls who are pregnant or parenting continue to be pushed out of school. These girls often face *discrimination, harassment, inflexible school policies, and other barriers, such as lack of childcare and transportation,*

which make it harder for them to remain and succeed in school. (National Women's Law Center, 2017)

More Educational Barriers

Here is a closer look at a few educational barriers pushing pregnant and parenting students out of school, and alongside each educational barrier are recommendations for how policy makers, administrators, teachers, counselors, and family/advocates can support pregnant and parenting students. Recommendations center on making sure the school is enforcing the law, but not just stopping there. Schools are urged to go beyond the basic legal requirements of the law and do everything they can to support pregnant and parenting students, thus fulfilling their commitment outlined in their vision and mission statements.

These recommendations come from the U.S. Department of Education, Office for Civil Rights (OCR) and the National Women's Law Center.

The OCR has published a pamphlet, *Supporting the Academic Success of Pregnant and Parenting Students* (2013), for administrators, teachers, and counselors on how to support pregnant and parenting students as they strive to finish their education. The pamphlet encourages schools to go beyond the legal requirement of Title IX to support pregnant and parenting students as they strive to finish school.

The National Women's Law Center has published recommendations for *Helping Girls Who Are Pregnant and Parenting Succeed in School* (National Women's Law Center, 2017). They offer recommendations for policy makers, schools, parents/guardians, and advocates.

Several of these recommendations from both the OCR and National Women's Law Center are discussed here in the context of how to address each educational barrier pushing pregnant and parenting students out of school. Educational barriers include:

1. Punitive absence and policies
2. Need for accommodations in school
3. Inaccessible homebound instruction
4. Stigma, bullying, harassment, and violence

Punitive Absence and Policies

Findings from *Let Her Learn* reveal that punitive absence policies can push girls who are pregnant or parenting out of school because they have to miss class for medical appointments, for their own medical recovery and needs and for when their children are ill or if their childcare arrangements fall through

- In the Let Her Learn Survey, girls who were pregnant or parenting (54 percent) were more likely than girls overall (25 percent) to report they had missed 15 days or more of school in a year.

Pregnant students need to miss school for medical appointments, childbirth, and recovery. They may also experience pregnancy-related nausea, exhaustion, and other ailments that do not require a doctor's visit but nevertheless make it hard to attend school. In the Let Her Learn Focus Groups, pregnant girls said that going to school while pregnant was physically challenging. In addition, a breastfeeding mother will need to be excused from class temporarily in order to express breast milk.

Student mothers can also find themselves in an impossible bind when their children are sick—send the child to daycare or miss school themselves. Many childcare facilities will not allow ill children to attend their programs until they have been symptom and fever free for twenty-four hours. As a result, a minor illness can keep a child out of daycare and a mother out of school for multiple days.

- Girls who are pregnant or parenting in the Let Her Learn Survey (91 percent) were more likely than girls overall (69 percent) to say that allowing special scheduling and attendance arrangements for students who provide care to family members would make schools better for girls.

Xiomara faced this situation in struggling to get herself and her daughter ready to arrive at school on time. To help pregnant and parenting students in this area, The OCR makes the following recommendations (*Supporting the Academic Success of Pregnant and Parenting Students Under Title IX of the Education Amendments of 1972*, 2013):

- Develop policies and procedures to address the needs of pregnant and parenting students. They recommend that if your school district does not already provide services such as at-home instruction for students who have temporary medical conditions, consider implementing policies to do so and remember that if homebound instruction is made available to students with temporary medical conditions, it must also be provided to pregnant students.
  - Allowing pregnant students to receive such support services could encourage them to remain in school.
  - Additionally, consider allowing excused absences for parenting students (both male and female) who need to take their children to doctors' appointments or to take care of their sick children.
  - By treating the absences as excused, you give these students the opportunity to make up the work they missed without being penalized, and you prevent them from falling behind.

It is important to note that in some cases, approving additional excused absences is out of the administrator's control. In some states, based on state law, a student can only miss ten days before failing. This is a policy change lawmakers would need to change to help pregnant and parenting students.

The NWLC offers recommendations for policy makers that are more appropriate when it comes to policies and procedures (National Women's Law Center, 2017). For example, the NWLC recommends that states pass laws and regulations that codify and expand upon Title IX's protections for girls who are pregnant or parenting. Specifically, states should:

- Require schools to excuse all pregnancy-related absences, including absences to recover from childbirth, as well as all absences necessary to care for an ill child.
- Require schools to provide pregnant and parenting students a reasonable amount of time to make up any missed work during excused absences.

Because these policies and practices are not currently in place, many pregnant and parenting students are being pushed out of school. To improve graduation rates for pregnant and parenting students, policy makers need to reevaluate attendance policies and make changes that will support pregnant and parenting students as they strive to complete their education.

Punitive absences and policies are not the only educational barriers that are pushing pregnant and parenting students out of school. The need for accommodations is another barrier.

Need for Accommodations in School

Another educational barrier that pregnant and parenting students face is the need for accommodations. Findings from *Let Her Learn* reveal that when schools refuse to make even simple accommodations for pregnant and parenting girls—such as providing extra time between classes or adjusting school uniforms—or worse, punish them for needing an accommodation, they make it harder for girls who are pregnant or parenting to succeed in school. Some schools have forced pregnant girls to sit at desks that are too small (National Women's Law Center, 2017).

Others have punished girls when their pregnancies made it harder for them to fulfill arbitrary requirements. For example, one school threatened a pregnant girl who no longer fit into her public school uniform with detention if she did not keep her shirt tucked in.

One girl in the Let Her Learn Focus Groups said that she was sent home or to detention when she did not complete her homework assignments on time: "It was kind of hard because sometimes I'll be too tired to do homework so I couldn't do it, and I was always in detention." Pushing pregnant and parenting students out of the classroom only makes it harder for them to keep up with their schoolwork and graduate.

The OCR recommends the type of assistance a school must provide a pregnant or parenting student (*Supporting the Academic Success of Pregnant and Parenting Students Under Title IX of the Education Amendments of 1972*, 2013).

- To ensure a pregnant student's access to its educational program, when necessary, a school must make adjustments to the regular

program that are reasonable and responsive to the student's temporary pregnancy status.
- For example, a school might be required to provide a larger desk, allow frequent trips to the bathroom, or permit temporary access to elevators.

The NWLC recommends that states pass laws and regulations that codify and expand upon Title IX's protections for girls who are pregnant or parenting (National Women's Law Center, 2017). Specifically, states should:

- Require schools to provide reasonable accommodations for pregnant and parenting students. For example, pregnant students may need to take extra time between classes or use the restroom more often.
- Require schools to allow breastfeeding students to express breastmilk or breastfeed their child during school.

The OCR recommends that schools consider asking pregnant and parenting students to share their views on ways that the school district can help them stay in school.

Inaccessible Homebound Instruction

There is yet another educational barrier pushing pregnant and parenting students out of school (National Women's Law Center, 2017). Findings from *Let Her Learn* also found that inaccessible homebound instruction was another educational barrier. Some girls who are pregnant or parenting may need homebound instruction or online learning opportunities but face barriers to accessing these services.

Some schools do not inform pregnant and parenting girls that homebound instruction exists and that they are eligible to participate. Pregnant girls also have been told that "normal" pregnancies do not qualify for homebound services. And only a handful of states require schools to offer homebound or online learning to students whose children have temporary illnesses or who are unable to attend school because they do not have access to childcare.

The Office for Civil Rights recommends that administrators prepare guidance materials to assist teachers, school nurses, counselors, and other staff in responding to the needs of pregnant and parenting students so they can stay in school (*Supporting the Academic Success of Pregnant and Parenting Students Under Title IX of the Education Amendments of 1972*, 2013).

The NWLC recommends that states pass laws and regulations that codify and expand upon Title IX's protections for girls who are pregnant or parenting. Specifically, states should (National Women's Law Center, 2017):

- Require schools to provide homebound instruction and/or access to online educational programs for pregnant or parenting students.

Having that homebound instruction is what helped Quincy, determined to finish her education. Were it not for that, she could have failed that year. If schools want to do all they can to help pregnant and parenting students graduate, they should be required to offer homebound instruction. This all goes back to a school's mission, vision, and core values/beliefs discussed in Chapter 1 and making sure efforts are made to ensure the success of pregnant and parenting students.

> "Becoming pregnant or having a child should not be the end of anyone's education. In fact, becoming a parent can be a powerful motivator that encourages young women to focus on their and their children's futures. Studies have found that student mothers who had previously disengaged from school can find new reasons to return after the birth of a child."
>
> —*Let Her Learn: Stopping School Pushout for Girls Who Are Pregnant and Parenting*
> National Women's Law Center

Stigma, Bullying, Harassment, and Violence

Other educational barriers were found that push pregnant and parenting students out of school (National Women's Law Center, 2017). One was stigma, bullying, harassment, and violence. According to data from *Let Her Learn*, negative life experiences such as violence, trauma, and homelessness can make it more likely that a teenage girl will become pregnant. At the same time, getting pregnant and becoming a parent also increases the likelihood that a girl will experience negative life events.

Being pregnant or a parent, for example, can make girls a target for unwanted sexual attention and harassment. According to the Let Her Learn Survey, girls who were pregnant or parenting were also more likely than girls overall to report that they had experienced harassment or violence of all kinds of violence."

The OCR (*Supporting the Academic Success of Pregnant and Parenting Students Under Title IX of the Education Amendments of 1972*, 2013), advises that harassing students is a violation of Title IX and notes:

- *Title IX* prohibits harassment of students based on sex, including harassment because of pregnancy or related conditions.
- Harassing conduct can take many forms, including verbal acts and name-calling, graphic and written statements, and other conduct that may be humiliating or physically threatening or harmful.
- Particular actions that could constitute prohibited harassment include making sexual comments or jokes about a student's pregnancy, calling a pregnant student sexually charged names, spreading rumors about her sexual activity, and making sexual propositions or gestures.
- Schools must take prompt and effective steps reasonably calculated to end pregnancy-related harassment, prevent its recurrence, and eliminate any hostile environment created by the harassment.
- The school violates *Title IX* if sexual harassment or other pregnancy-related harassment by employees, students, or third parties is sufficiently serious that it interferes with a student's ability to benefit from or participate in the school's program, and the harassment is encouraged, tolerated, not adequately addressed, or ignored by school employees.

Two graduates, Xiomara and Renee, experienced harassment and bullying, and they were not protected. Xiomara felt she had no other choice than to go to the alternative school because she didn't want "to be jumped" again by girls who had already been harassing her. Kelly endured harassment with another girl wanting to fight her because of her boyfriend.

> I had a lot of drama in high school. Me and the father of my child, we were together—we got together in middle school, and I was in the seventh grade. We had been together for a long time, even until my freshman year in college, but it was just a lot of drama. At first, we weren't together when I got into high school, but then we got back together. Then it was some girl, he would always be like, "Oh, she's just my friend. She's just my friend." I come to find out he was having sex with her, cheating on me with her, the whole time I was pregnant, as I had my baby and everything, just a hot mess.
>
> The girl was telling people she was going to fight me after I had my baby, but ain't never fight me, ain't never said nothing out of her way to me or whatever, just being a punk. I remember the day before I was induced, I was in the hallway, talking to him. It was at the school, and she was there, too, the girl he was cheating on me with. She was there, too. I just remember blanking on him and all this stuff, showing out at the school in the hallways. At the end of it, he walked away with her, with his arm around her neck.

Threats of "being jumped" and "harassment from girls wanting to fight you" are a violation of Title IX and pregnant and parenting students' protection against harassment. To protect the rights of pregnant and parenting students, the OCR recommends schools:

- Have the *Title IX* coordinator provide training to students to ensure that they know that *Title IX* prohibits harassment of students based on sex, including harassment because of pregnancy or related conditions and *Title IX* prohibits discrimination against pregnant and parenting students. (*Supporting the Academic Success of Pregnant and Parenting Students Under Title IX of the Education Amendments of 1972*, 2013)

Summary

Title IX was designed to protect a pregnant and parenting student's right to an education and while it is illegal to expel or dismiss students, educational barriers exist that push pregnant and parenting students out of school, despite protection under Title IX. Educational barriers like:

1. Punitive absence and policies
2. Need for accommodations in school
3. Inaccessible homebound instruction
4. Stigma, bullying, harassment, and violence

To help pregnant and parenting students graduate, schools must ensure that students are not discriminated against. Schools must ensure their rights under Title IX are protected. They must ensure that the educational barriers exist at their school that push pregnant and parenting students out of school are addressed. Schools must ensure they fulfill their commitment in their vision and mission statement. Fulfilling their obligations to this student population will help pregnant and parenting students graduate.

Special Note: LGBTQI Youth and Pregnancy

A special note must be made regarding LGBTQI youth and pregnancy. The *Oxford Dictionary* defines LGBTQI as "lesbian, gay, bisexual, transgender, queer (or questioning), and intersex."

The National Women's Law Center, in March 2022, published *A Call to Action to Support LGBTQI Pregnant, Expectant, and Parenting Students*. The report notes:

- A growing body of research indicates that when compared to straight teens, bisexual teen girls are more likely to become pregnant. In one study from 2018, bisexual teen girls were five times more likely that straight teen girls to become pregnant before age twenty.
- Research on lesbian teen pregnancy is mixed—one study found lesbian girls were half as likely as heterosexual girls to become

pregnant, while two other studies found lesbian girls were more likely than heterosexual girls to become pregnant.
- Studies have found transgender youth are just as likely to become pregnant as cisgender youth. Some teens with intersex traits can also become pregnant, though less is known about this population.
- The center's research found that like straight pregnant and parenting students, trauma, and adverse childhood experiences plague LGBTQI teens.
- The report says that these teens, "feel increased pressure to conform to heterosexuality and gender norms and "prove" that they are straight and cisgender, particularly if they experience bullying or other harassment based on their identity.
- Students who are bullied are more likely to become pregnant as a teen, and LGBTQI students experience bullying at higher rates than their non-LGBTQI peers. In 2019, over a third of LGB (40%) students reported having been bullied at school in the last year, compared to 22% of straight students.
- Likewise, according to the 2015 U.S. Transgender Survey, over half (54%) of respondents reported experiencing verbal harassment while in school because they were transgender.
- LGBTQI students of color face intersecting forms of bullying and harassment, with over half of Latinx, AAPI, and Black LGBTQ students, and 65% of Native and Indigenous LGBTQ students reporting that they felt unsafe in school because of their sexual orientation, according to a 2015 survey conducted by GLSEN."
- More alarming and indicative of why educators, school administrators and parents must assure that Title IX is being enforced is that "In addition to being more likely to experience bullying, LGBTQI students are more likely to experience sexual violence than straight, cisgender students, which also increases the likelihood of pregnancy."
- In 2019, more than one in five LGB students reported being the victim of sexual violence at least once during the past year, compared to 9% of straight students. In 2017, 23% of transgender students reported being forced to have sexual intercourse compared to 12% of cisgender female students and 3.5% of cisgender male students.

- Overall, pregnant teens are more likely to have experienced sexual abuse than teens who do not become pregnant.

So the educational barriers that push pregnant and parenting students out of school are also impacting LGBTQI students. Schools must ensure the school climate is safe for these students and protect them from harassment.

Blatant Violations—The Pregnant Scholar

Title IX has likely not decreased the dropout rate for pregnant and parenting teens because schools are blatantly violating the law. Some examples were noted above regarding the stigma, bullying, harassment, and violence pregnant and parenting students face.

An example of a school, in this case a university, blatantly violating Title IX is what happened to a pregnant student in the second semester of her senior year (*Pregnant Scholar Profiles: Kamaria Downs*, 2017). When Kamaria Downs was a senior in college, her university evicted her from student housing because she was pregnant—a violation of Title IX's prohibition on discrimination based on pregnancy.

Kamaria successfully challenged the university's rules with help from attorneys at Public Justice and Correia & Puth. As a result, the university revoked its discriminatory housing policy, created new housing and anti-discrimination policies to support pregnant and parenting students, agreed to hire new Title IX personnel, and expanded its Title IX training and outreach for students and staff.

The Pregnant Scholar, which profiled the student, provides an excerpt of Kamaria sharing her struggle, her victory, and advice for others in a similar situation (*Pregnant Scholar Profiles: Kamaria Downs*, 2017):

> *When did you have your daughter? What did you expect it would be like to be pregnant in college?*
>
> I was a senior and I was in my last semester when the entire ordeal happened. I had always intended to finish my degree. I never had a doubt in my mind about graduating.

What was your university's response to your pregnancy?

The University found out [I was pregnant] when I went to student teach and they had a form that I had to fill out to disclose any and all of my medical information. Evidently that information wasn't kept confidential. My dean called me into her office a few days after I submitted the form, and she was telling me that I'd have to move out because I was pregnant. . . .

Nobody else confronted me about it until a couple of months later when I was called into the housing coordinator's office. She asked me if I was pregnant, and I told her "yes." She basically told me the same thing: "You know, you're going to have to move out because you're pregnant." At that point I was just telling her, "Give me a few days to find some living arrangements."

Thankfully, I had been in a conversation with my professor/mentor because she knew they were going to drop the ball on me. She opened up her home to me and let me know that if I needed to stay there with her I could.

What led to your decision to challenge the policy against pregnant women in dorms?

After graduation I actually took a year off to be with my daughter—and just sitting there enjoying her, watching her grow every day and change every day, it made me realize that in the beginning I was literally concealing my pregnancy from everyone just because I was afraid of what the university would do. It made me realize that I didn't get to enjoy my pregnancy, and it isn't right.

It's not right for me to feel shamed for being pregnant just because I'm unmarried, or just because I'm still in college—that doesn't matter. And so I wanted to prevent it from happening to other people. I wanted to prevent another woman from feeling as ashamed of her pregnancy as I did.

Unfortunately, it still happened to some other people after I graduated, but at this point I'm sure it's not happening anymore!

Once you came forward, what was the response like?

I logged into my university email . . . when the settlement was finally made, and I saw the email that they sent out to the entire university thanking me for coming forward with my story and helping to change the policy to make it equal for all people within the university.

And [I saw] the response for an interview I'd done—a ton of my friends shared the link, and everyone has been telling me how proud they are of me for standing up for what is right. Overall, the response has been very good, and I'm so excited about it. And I'm very appreciative that [the university] made the changes that they did.

What advice would you give to other pregnant students?

I would just say that it is still possible to graduate; don't doubt yourself or what you can do! Think about your children; you're doing this for them. And I would just say, to anybody, know your Title IX rights.

What about professors, any advice on how they can support pregnant students?

Be open to change. I know a lot of universities have a policy against pregnant and parenting students, but you have to be open to everyone and be able to accommodate them. It's wrong to treat people the way I was treated. Instead, provide avenues for them to finish their degree and be able to take their classes without any hassles or having them go through the runaround to get things done.

Just be helpful to those in need, and don't look down upon them. I feel like that's how it was at my university. A lot of leaders and administrators looked down on me because I'm unmarried, I'm pregnant, I'm still in college. Don't be condemning of people, don't look down on them; that's the worst thing possible.

You've now graduated; what are you and your daughter up to?

She is one year old. She is so smart and full of energy and everything I could've wished for. I am currently teaching 2nd grade in Greenville, South Carolina. And I'm in my first year. It has been my dream to be a teacher, and now I'm actually waking up and living that dream while at the same time having my family and just enjoying life.

This student's ordeal is an example of a blatant violation of the law. The university violated Kamaria's rights to an education under Title IX. This occurred even after Kamaria's professor/mentor brought the violation to the attention of the housing administration. Unfortunately, the housing administration of the university ignored her concerns.

Was this because the university didn't think anything would come of it? Was it that they thought they could get away with it? Was it just that Title IX's application to pregnant and parenting students wasn't on their radar? No one knows, but what is unfortunate is that, just as this student's university blatantly violated her rights, there is a very real possibility that other blatant violations of Title IX are going on in plain sight. Many schools who receive federal funds may be violating pregnant and parenting students' rights under the law—without reprimand. This is likely because pregnant and parenting students don't know their rights, so they don't know they can challenge the university's actions. They don't have someone like Kamaria's professor/mentor to make them aware of their rights.

Such violations are pushing pregnant and parenting students out of school and contributing to the 50 percent push out rate. The outcome for Kamaria could have been vastly different if she had not been able to finish the second semester of her senior year. Had she dropped out because the university pushed her out when they forced her move out of the dorm—and did not provide any alternative accommodations or a housing refund—she would not be the teacher she dreamed of being and not be able to care for her daughter as she does. This is why Title IX has not worked for many pregnant and parenting students. Students are pushed out of school because schools are blatantly violating this federal law. To help pregnant and parenting students graduate, schools must enforce the law.

SUMMARY

Prior to Title IX, pregnant and parenting students were expelled or dismissed from school with no recourse. They were denied the right to an education. The passage of Title IX made such discrimination illegal. Title IX has been credited with decreasing the dropout rate of high school girls, but this success does not hold true for pregnant and parenting students. Yet, fifty years after Title IX was enacted, the dropout rate for pregnant and parenting students is 50 percent. Title IX has not worked for these students.

Many factors contribute to why Title IX has not decreased the dropout rate. Two of them are educational barriers that push students out of school and blatant violations of the law. To decrease the dropout rate, and help pregnant and parenting students graduate, schools must enforce the law.

NOTE

1. *This Day in History*, June 23, 1972. Retrieved from History.com. https://www.history.com/this-day-in-history/title-ix-enacted

CHAPTER 3

Support from Home Matters

New mothers have a mountain of stories colorfully painting the angst, stress, overwhelm, inadequate hours and inadequate rest endured by the presence of one tiny new person in their lives. Imagine, then, the multiplication of that when the new mother is a student in high school or early college—the concerns intensified by research papers, final exams, peer pressure, homework, and the desire to maintain a sense of normalcy as a young woman. Without support from an integral community—family—the trauma of their new role as mom increases. In this chapter you will read how support from home is vital in helping pregnant and parenting students graduate and learn about alternative viable options for those who don't have support at home.

Schools alone cannot address all the challenges pregnant and parenting students face. The meaningful involvement of parents and support from home are essential. Support from home, particularly from a strong female family role model, was top of the list of reasons for graduates' success. For several participants, it was due to the presence of their mother and/or grandmother that they graduated.

Quincy celebrates the way her grandmother helped her see beyond her bump in the road.

> If I were handing out awards, I would give the all-star award to my grandmother. She's been there for me, no matter how upset she was when she found out I was pregnant. She's provided everything for me. If I needed it, it was there. If my child needed it, it was there. And she pushed me. She was the reason I never gave up. She would always tell me, "You give up, then you getting out my house."

Quincy's grandmother's support is a banner example of how village elders can become the catalyst to face challenges and overcome them.

She would keep me going. She would say, "Don't come in my house with any Fs, don't come in my house with any Ds. If the class is too hard, you can C your way out, but you're not going to D and F your way out." That was always her motto. She even went back to school because I was in school. She told me that if she can go back to school and pass some classes, I can stay in school and pass my classes. Her point was, "If I can do it, you can do it."

> "If I were handing out awards, I would give the all-star award to my grandmother. She's been there for me, no matter how upset she was when she found out I was pregnant. She's provided everything for me. If I needed it, it was there. If my child needed it, it was there."
>
> —Quincy, a graduate and college student

With an invitation to attend a prominent HBCU in hand, Toni was faced with a dilemma. Could she do it and parent at the same time? Support from her mom, from home, assured that she absolutely could if she desired it.

Me and my parents sat down, and we're like, "Well what are we going to do?" And my mom, she automatically said, "Well, the child's going to stay here." And that was the best thing. I love the fact—the things that older parents teach, instill in the children, was there. It was there. And my side, I don't necessarily know—you're growing up. You're trying to understand how to raise a child. Still, it was hard. It was hard for me to go off to school and leave my son.

Planning and management became the strategies employed to help ease Toni's concerns, assure her son would be cared for physically and financially, and alleviate the question of whether Toni could concentrate on school.

A program I was in provided me with childcare assistance, which means I could still put my son in daycare. What my mother is doing is taking care of him day in and day out, but I'm not taking her money for my child. Financially, I supported him. I was actually sending money back for him. So anything that he might have needed between me and his father we supplied it. My mother didn't have to do the financial piece. We set him up in the perfect situation. Having a child young is not the ideal situation, but my situation turned out perfectly.

Toni's mom helped her in another way—with her internal struggle of being away from her son. When she worried about abandoning her son, *her mother* would bring her back, saying, "No, this is good for him."

> So she [my mother] was definitely there. Her and my dad were instrumental in raising him, and what I didn't understand at that point—I felt—what's the word? I felt like I was abandoning him.
>
> And going on through the years, the four years that I was there, I used to talk to my mother a lot about that. And she would bring me back, said, "No, this is beneficial for him."
>
> And jumping ahead, after I finished school, my son was now four going on five. I asked him, I said, "Do you know that mommy went off to school?" And he said, "No." So everything that I feared didn't even come true.

So the support of a strong female presence helped students graduate. For Quincy it was her grandmother; for Toni it was her mother.

Just like Quincy and Toni, for Diane, support from home helped her graduate. When asked who helped her graduate, her response was "my mom."

> [If] it wasn't for my mom, to be honest with you, I don't think I would have finished high school. She got pregnant at 16 and she had to get her GED, and she said, "You know, you're not going to go that route. She said, "You know, you might be pregnant, but you're not going to get your GED; you're going to get your high school diploma." And she pushed me every day. "You okay? You feeling okay? Go ahead and go to school. Get it out the way. God's got something for you. Just get up and go." She really pushed me. If I didn't have that support system, I don't think I would have finished high school.

> "[If] it wasn't for my mom, to be honest with you, I don't think I would have finished high school. . . . She really pushed me. If I didn't have that support system, I don't think I would have finished high school."
>
> —Diane, a graduate and college student

For Quincy, Toni, and Diane, it was the support of their mother or grandmother that helped them graduate. Because of a strong female supporter, they were able to face their external and internal struggles and overcome them.

WHY SUPPORT FROM HOME MATTERS

Support from home matters because many problems pregnant and parenting students face are on the home front—problems at home like getting adequate sleep and time management. Families can help alleviate these real struggles. Several graduates attested to this.

Renee learned the hard way that simply closing her eyes and resting was more significant than she could have imagined.

> Trying to get enough sleep and trying to manage my time with school and my daughter was a major challenge. That's one reason I'm happy my mom was there, because when I tried to do my homework, she was helping me by holding my child. But then—going to sleep because my daughter go to sleep so late. She would wake up so early. It was just a struggle. My mother, on my school nights, if my little girl was still up past ten, she would take her from me, and she would say, "I'm going to try to put her to bed. You've got to go to bed because I've got to get up early in the morning."

For Xiomara, time was also problematic. Yet, for her, it was more about being able to rise and shine in a punctual manner. Her experience was compounded by unsympathetic staff, even in a school setting designed for pregnant and parenting students

> I had to wake up every two hours on the hour to feed her, and then wake up and get her ready for school and get me ready for school and then go

to school. I was late all the time! The lady at school who sat there to let you sign the late paper when you come in would be fussing at me. I'm like, "It's not me, it's her. She's not cooperative in the morning." She would tell me, "Well, you've got to tell her you've got to get to school on time."

Unfortunately, those multiple tardy listings were seen as penalties, possibly in violation of Title IX exceptions, and nearly resulted in Xiomara failing school that year.

Time management was also a struggle for Alger. As she transitioned into cosmetology school, support from home helped her manage going to school and being a mom.

> It's definitely time management and it's also putting your best foot forward on your worst day. When you're raising a child, you want to be able to teach them and spend time with them, just be the best mother. That is a huge struggle for me. It does become overwhelming at times, and my mom does give moral support. Some people don't have that. I have my mom and my immediate family that does support.

So the challenges Renee, Xiomara, and Alger faced were all at home. Their families helped them manage their challenges and are powerful examples of why support from home and family is so important.

Another graduate, Kelly, was dealing with the drama of her cheating boyfriend. When asked who helped her overcome that challenge, it was *her mom*:

> My mom would be like, "Don't worry about that girl, don't worry about that thing." She would tell me stuff that I know now is true. She would try to tell me when I was younger, but I really wasn't trying to listen. She would tell me, "You deserve better than that. It'd really go out one ear, but she was always there, telling me, "Don't let that stuff bother you."

> "It [managing it all] does become overwhelming at times, and my mom does give moral support. Some people don't have that. I have my mom and my immediate family that does support."
>
> —Alger, a graduate and college student

Often pregnant and parenting students are afraid to tell their parents that they are pregnant, out of fear of disappointing them. Thus, they conceal their pregnancy for as long as they can. Hiding her pregnancy was Diane's temporary solution to not facing her parents. Although she had spoken to a trusted teacher and the school nurse, disclosing the information to her parents introduced a world of anxiety driven by assured disappointment.

> I kind of started showing a little. And I got a note sent home because my test score was a little low. They had to sign it. And she (my mom) was like, "This isn't like you. What's going on?" And I started crying, and it just came out. And she (my mom) screamed! They screamed and yelled at me! And she was like, "You better wobble yourself across that stage."

Diane's mother's response was consistent with what she feared, and she felt even worse knowing she had disappointed her mom. But Diane's mother quickly came around. She accepted her daughter's reality and provided her the support she needed so she could graduate. As Diane said, "[If] It wasn't for my mom, to be honest with you, I don't think I would have finished high school."

So, students were able to graduate because they had support from home. For Quincy it was her grandmother. For Toni, Xiomara, Diane, and Alger it was their mother. Support from home is critical for pregnant and parenting students to graduate, and that is the problem for many pregnant and parenting students do not complete high school: they don't have that support from home.

No Support from Home

The problem for many pregnant and parenting students who do not complete high school is they don't have a lot of support from home. They don't have a grandmother like Quincy's who will be there and provide for what they and their child need. They don't have a mother like Toni's who will keep their child so they can go to college. They don't have a mother like Diane's who will push them. They don't have that kind of support, and that hinders their academic success. Pregnant and parenting students likely don't have that support because they are caught in an intergenerational cycle of teen pregnancy.

Caught in an Intergenerational Cycle

In large numbers, pregnant and parenting students are also products of a teen mom and part of a continuing family cycle. Often this cycle includes the traumas of the previous generation. When left unaddressed and unhealed, the impact of the trauma and the pervasiveness of the trauma continues.

If you go back one generation and trace the mother's story, likely you will find her story was part of that collective story of pregnant and parenting students—a life riddled with violence, abuse, ACEs, psychological damage, depression and anxiety, and substance abuse. Here's how her story might read:

As a teen mom, she was part of the two-thirds of adolescent mothers who were sexually and/or physically abused and part of the 50 to 80 percent who are in a violent or abusive relationship before, during or after her teen pregnancy (Leiderman & Almo, 2001). She became a teen mom, pregnant directly or indirectly from the prior abuse, violence, and the ACEs she experienced in her childhood. She may have become pregnant directly from that interpersonal violence through sexual abuse, incest, or birth control sabotage. She might have become pregnant indirectly because the psychological damage of that prior abuse made her more susceptible to coercive and abusive partners and at a greater risk for teen pregnancy.

As a teen mom, she may have been one of the young mothers who suffered from depression and anxiety. She may have self-medicated with drugs and alcohol. She may have been in a relationship with a controlling partner and, within one year, had a repeat pregnancy as the research shows—pregnant and parenting students give birth to another child within a year and a half.

As a student herself, she faced some of the educational barriers that push pregnant and parenting student out of school (National Women's Law Center, 2017). Barriers like those already discussed: an environment of discouragement; lack of support; and stigma, bullying, harassment, and violence.

She may have endured the same judgment and shame that Xiomara, Quincy, and Alger spoke of. If a school environment of discouragement was too much to bear, with her crushed spirit and no support, she became part of the 50 percent of pregnant and parenting students who are pushed out of school and do not earn a high school diploma. (*Reproductive Health: Teen Pregnancy*, 2021).

The pervasiveness of violence and abuse in her life put her daughter—the pregnant or parenting student sitting in your classroom—at a high risk for difficulties. The result is the negative outcomes for children of teen mothers.

According to Youth.gov, children who are born to teen mothers experience a wide range of problems (*Pregnancy Prevention: The Adverse Effects of Teen Pregnancy*, n.d.). For example, they are more likely to:

- have a higher risk for low birth weight and infant mortality;
- have lower levels of emotional support and cognitive stimulation;
- have fewer skills and be less prepared to learn when they enter kindergarten;
- have behavioral problems and chronic medical conditions;
- rely more heavily on publicly funded health care;
- have higher rates of foster care placement;
- be incarcerated at some time during adolescence;
- have lower school achievement and drop out of high school;
- give birth as a teen; and
- be unemployed or underemployed as a young adult.

So, now facing a teen pregnancy, the pregnant or parenting student sitting in your class comes with many of the challenges above. She is caught in an intergenerational cycle of teen pregnancy.

Because many pregnant and parenting students are caught in that cycle of teen pregnancy, they don't have a mother at home who can support them, who can push them like Diane's mom, and they end up not completing high school. For those pregnant and parenting students with limited support from home, what are they to do? How do they get the support from home that is so vital?

There are viable options for pregnant and parenting students who don't have support from home. They include:

- A surrogate mother figure who steps up
- Fathers must take on their responsibility
- A residential academy

A Surrogate Mother Figure

For pregnant and parenting students who don't have support from their mother, to help them graduate, the best option is for a surrogate mother figure to step up and help her. This person could be an aunt, cousin, or family friend. It could be a grandmother—like Quincy's grandmother (because her mom was addicted to drugs and alcohol). It can even be a teacher—which will be discussed in the next chapter.

This person can help the pregnant or parenting student as she strives to finish school. A surrogate mother figure can help buy what she needs for herself and her child. That's what Quincy's grandmother did: provided what she and her child needed. A surrogate mother can ensure the pregnant and parenting student is taking advantage of all available resources in the community and government assistance programs while she's in school.

A surrogate mother figure can be a source of emotional support for the pregnant or parenting student who might be in an abusive relationship. This is what Kelly's mother was to her—a source of encouragement. The surrogate mother can encourage her and help her understand that she deserves better.

A surrogate mother figure can ensure that the pregnant and parenting students' Title IX rights are not being violated. She can be her advocate if she is being bullied or harassed at school. She can help her file a complaint with the Title IX coordinator at her school or the U.S. Department of Education, Office for Civil Rights. A surrogate mother figure can offer the much-needed support from home that pregnant and parenting students need to graduate.

The challenge with a surrogate mother is that she lives outside the home. Because she is not in the home, she's not able to help the pregnant or parenting student with real daily struggles like getting adequate sleep and managing it all. That was Renee's and Xiomara's challenge—just getting enough sleep and managing it all. Renee was able to rest because her mom and brother helped her. So this is one challenge with a surrogate mother figure who steps up: she is not living in the home.

Another problem is the family dynamics that pregnant and parenting students come from. If there is a cycle of abuse, violence, and teen pregnancy, adults function using a lot of maladaptive coping strategies, like having boundary issues, co-dependent behaviors, abandonment issues, conflict resolution issues, and trauma-related disorders—depression, anxiety disorders, PTSD, and addiction.

This places the teen mom in a victim stance, where she feels she has little control over her life and cannot say no. Consequently, she must do what her family says and accept however she is treated—because she needs their support—and often she is controlled and manipulated by the same family members who say they love and support her.

There is a lot of judgment and shame that is part of their family dynamics. Pregnant and parenting students are treated as a disgrace, and some have even been told that they "embarrassed the family." Xiomara and Alger faced a wave of judgment from their families. They found out that family is not always where they could receive unconditional love and support.

For Xiomara, even though she had excelled in school, her teen pregnancy caused her family to look down on her. Through tears, she talked about attending college, disappointing her family, and facing a family that viewed her differently and negatively. Yet she was driven to redeem herself and restore their positive perception of her.

She felt that when she graduated from college, they would say, "She really did it." She didn't let a teen pregnancy hold her back:

> I feel great about attending college because I know that it's going to open up doors for us in the future, and I feel that all the people who are disappointed and are let down, I feel like some way this would reaffirm me and let them know that even though I did make a mistake—not saying [my daughter] is a mistake, but teenage pregnancy was a mistake—that I'm still the same Xiomara that y'all are used to. I'm still smart, I'm still going to finish school like y'all expected me to from the beginning.

Even with such resolve, Xiomara admits her family's strong disappointment did damage her self-esteem:

> My dad's side of the family—they always put me on a pedestal. And even on my mom's side of the family, they always put me on a pedestal just because I was so smart, and because I always got straight A's. When I got pregnant—like everybody just—I guess looked at me a different type of way. And I know—I want to cry.
>
> But I know that I'm the same Xiomara that they're used to—but I care a lot about what my family thinks about me, and I just feel like I let them down so much by getting pregnant, and I just ruined their whole perception of me. I want to get that back. I want them to look at me the same way. I feel like at my college graduation is when they're going to say, "She really did it. She really didn't let this hold her back."

As for Alger, she felt some family members judged her:

> I had some family members that were negative. I do come from a close, a very, very close family, but we also have a lot of other people, and they think of the way it's supposed to be done; you're supposed to get married and have a baby and do everything traditional. Considering the fact that I didn't do it that way, I was judged by that, and a lot of people thought that I wasn't going to make it, just because I didn't go the correct route.

It's understandable that families are not happy about a teen pregnancy. No one is going to be happy about a teen pregnancy. None of the graduates were, but that was their reality. They couldn't change it, and what pregnant and parenting students need is someone from home—if not their mother, then a surrogate mother figure—to believe in them, support them, and keep encouraging them.

The graduates' experiences illustrate how support from home matters because many of the real struggles pregnant and parenting students face are at home. For graduates, a strong female role model was their source of support. This was either their mom or grandmother. Pregnant and parenting students who drop out, don't have that support. Still, support from home matters.

If the pregnant and parenting student's mom is not that source of support and encouragement, the next viable option is for a surrogate mother figure to step in that role. This surrogate mother figure can be a source of hope and inspiration. She can ensure the teen mom's Title IX rights are protected. There are challenges with having a surrogate mother figure who is a family member, and because home support is so important, this issue must be addressed.

Fathers Must Take on Their Responsibility

The next critical component pregnant and parenting students need so they can graduate is for their child's father to take on his responsibility. Among graduates, only one father was actively involved. He was involved in his child's life and provided financial support to care for his child. Pregnant and parenting students need support from the other parent, and the father is just as responsible for financially supporting his child. Without the support of the father, pregnant and parenting students are on their own. They struggle to pay for childcare because they have no financial support. Alger, though blessed with multifaceted support from her mother everything financial was on her.

> My mother is definitely there for me to talk to, but when it comes to financials, I totally financed everything for myself. I don't have anyone that I can call to say, "Do you have it this week?" because if I don't have it, then it doesn't get done. I don't get any financial support from my son's father, not at all. I pay for daycare, through a full-time job. And I still have to get things, and then I still have to work. He has to go to daycare, but luckily, he's in a home daycare, so the people that keep him have been keeping him since he's been six weeks. They're flexible with us, but the prices don't change.

Alger's struggle is why the father must support his child. He needs to provide for the daily care of his child and provide financial support. Financial support is critical. It can help with childcare—a major challenge for parenting students trying to finish school.

Fathers can voluntarily take on their responsibility or if they do not, they can be legally required to care for their child. If the father is under age 18, then the responsibility to support the child falls to his parents. In terms of child support, Women's Law notes the following (*North Carolina, Child Support, When Parent Is a Minor*, 2022):

> If *both parents* are under 18 (and unemancipated) at the time of the child's conception, *their parents* (the child's grandparents) *share pri-*

mary responsibility for supporting the child. This responsibility lasts until *both* minor unemancipated parents become age 18 or are emancipated.

If only one parent was under 18 (and unemancipated) at the time of the child's conception and the other parent was over 18, the over-18 parent has *primary responsibility* to support the child for his/her share and the *grandparents of the under-18* (unemancipated) parent shares primary responsibility for his/her share of the child support. However, if the over-18 parent does not pay, and owes past-due child support (called "arrearages"), *all of the grandparents are liable for arrearages* (past-due support) until the minor parent reaches the age of 18 or becomes emancipated. (*North Carolina, Child Support, When Parent Is a Minor,* 2022)

Again, fathers can voluntarily take care of their responsibility. If they do not, there is a legal recourse that needs to be followed. They are just as responsible for the day-to-day responsibilities of caring for their child and providing financial support. Pregnant and parenting students need fathers to do their share as the mother endeavors to complete her education.

A problem is that often fathers are not employed or may fail to keep a steady job and often they don't know how to be a father because they did not have a role model. They didn't have a father. They don't know how to be a responsible father or what that looks like. They too are likely caught in an intergenerational cycle of fathers who are absent and not in their child's life.

This is where community organizations geared toward supporting young fathers to be active in their child's life play a pivotal role. Fathers can learn what it means to be a father from these organizations so that they are able to be the father they need to be for their child. Pregnant and parenting students need that. They need fathers to take on their responsibility.

But what if neither is an option? What if there is no surrogate mother figure to step in, and the father doesn't step up to take care of his responsibility? What if he doesn't provide for the daily needs of his child, and he doesn't provide financially. What then happens to the parenting mother? She ends up not being able to complete high school, and there is no easy solution to this. This is evidenced by the 50 percent dropout rate that this has improved over the years. Fifty years after Title IX there is still a major crisis in the dropout rate for pregnant and parenting students.

A Residential Academy

There is a solution, though, to solving the many challenges pregnant and parenting students face. It would be a huge undertaking and would require significant and sustainable financial support, but it could change the entire trajectory of a teen mom's life and her child's. Along with educating students and their child, it could literally be the catalyst for real, sustainable change.

The best option to decrease the dropout rate for pregnant and parenting students and to reengage those who have dropped out is a residential academy for pregnant and parenting students and their children. This would be a place they can call home for the period needed to complete their education, develop interpersonal skills, and develop employment skills. A residential academy would solve a major challenge for pregnant and parenting students and their children: adequate housing for moms.

This residential location, using evidence-based practices to help the mom complete her education, provides high-quality childcare. At this residential location, she can develop interpersonal and work skills. She can begin to heal from the adverse experiences in her life.

The *Interpersonal Violence and Adolescent Pregnancy* report stresses the critical need for parents to heal from their own violent experiences, so they can support the healthy emotional development of their children (Leiderman & Almo, 2001). If they don't heal, it will be challenge for them to attach (attachment is so important) and meet the emotional needs of their child. Realistically, for pregnant and parenting students to heal, they must be pulled out of their chaotic home environment where adults function using maladaptive coping skills like co-dependent behaviors and boundary issues.

This is what happens at the Oprah Winfrey Leadership Academy (OWLAG) in South Africa.[1] Girls are taken out of their chaotic home environment where they had endured lots of ACEs, and they are put in a healthy environment where they can thrive. In terms of ACEs, the founder, Oprah Winfrey, has spoken on how she brought in Dr. Bruce Perry, a leading expert on childhood trauma and brain development, to address a situation where girls were disassociating in class. Dissociation is often the result of enduring lots of Adverse Childhood Experiences (ACEs) which are prevalent in the lives of teen moms and their children. Winfrey has noted in interviews that the average ACEs score for girls at her leadership academy is 6. Teen moms who share a collective story of violence and abuse likely have a high ACEs score too.

Pregnant and parenting students are coming from that same kind of chaotic and stressful environment, and to provide them with the comprehensive support and resources they need, the answer is a residential academy—a safe place they can call home with their child for four or five years.

Harlem Children's Zone

This residential academy could function much like the Harlem Children's Zone (HCZ)[2] in Harlem, founded by Geoffrey Canada, a renowned thought leader and passionate advocate for education reform. The Harlem Children's Zone is a nonprofit organization that started as a movement to transform central Harlem. It has grown into a vision for breaking the cycle of intergenerational poverty across the world. For pregnant and parenting students, caught in the cycle of teen pregnancy, they are in a cycle of intergenerational poverty.

The Harlem Children's Zone project began as a one-block pilot in the 1990s. Then and still today, it exists to provide comprehensive, critical support to children and families in order to reweave the very fabric of community life. With bold ambition, careful planning, and a strong infrastructure, they set out to address not just some, but *all* of the issues children and families face—crumbling apartments, rampant drug use, failing schools, violent crime, and chronic health problems—both in central Harlem and everywhere.

This is what pregnant and parenting students and their children need. A residential academy that addresses not just some, but *all of* the challenges they face.

On its website, HCZ notes that since its founding, its pioneering place-based model has grown in scale and serves more than 22,500 children and families annually within their 97-block zone. Their impact has garnered global attention—they have hosted thought leaders and partnered with organizations from across the United States and over two hundred countries that seek guidance on how to replicate the model. The HCZ provides services from early childhood through college. As part of their Early Childhood Program, they offer:

- The Baby College
- Three-Year-Old Journey
- Harlem Gems

They run Promise Academy Charter Schools. At Promise Academy Charter Schools, they do whatever it takes to get their scholars to and through college. This is exactly the kind of village and community care pregnant and parenting students need for themselves and their children.

Oprah Winfrey Leadership Academy for Girls in South Africa

A residential school could offer the services of the Harlem Children's Zone but could resemble the Oprah Winfrey Leadership Academy for Girls in South Africa.[3] OWLAG is a school dedicated to combating poverty through education. This is what a residential school for pregnant and parenting students would do—make a tremendous impact in combating poverty through education.

The Oprah Winfrey Foundation notes on its website that the concept for the OWLAG began with a conversation with South African president Nelson Mandela. In 2002, Oprah Winfrey and President Mandela were talking about combating poverty. Winfrey, who was staying at the president's home, said she believes education is the key to leveling the playing field—and revealed she intended to one day build a school for girls in the country. Mandela immediately jumped into action to make sure that day was as soon as possible. Just five years later, the OWLAG opened its doors.

The Foundation notes that each student has had to overcome childhood poverty and trauma during their lives, yet also possesses a resilience, courage, and spirit that make them stand out among their peers.

Winfrey, who was born into poverty in the Jim Crow South, says, "I wanted to build a school for girls like me." Ironically and realistically, a school for pregnant and parenting students would be "a school for girls like her." She herself endured trauma in her childhood that resulted in a teen pregnancy.

A residential school for pregnant and parenting students would eliminate several more educational barriers that push girls out of school. The findings from *Let Her Learn: Stopping School Pushout for Girls Who Are Pregnant or Parenting* revealed a few remaining educational barriers that pregnant and parenting students face (National Women's Law Center, 2017):

1. Lack of childcare
2. Need for transportation
3. Stress, insufficient time, and the need to work
4. Economic, housing, and family instability

These barriers would be eliminated with a residential academy where pregnant and parenting students live for a period of time with their children and are provided the kinds of services that the Harlem Children's Zone offers.

Lack of Childcare

A major challenge for pregnant and parenting students that a residential academy could overcome is lack of childcare. Results from *Let Her Learn* found that student mothers consistently report that they lack accessible and affordable childcare, which is necessary for them to succeed in school—not only so they can attend school but also so they can work (National Women's Law Center, 2017).

Childcare that extends beyond the students' school day can also give the parent needed time to complete schoolwork or participate in school activities. Girls in the Let Her Learn Focus Groups reported that having to care for their children made it harder for them to complete their homework.

- More than half of girls (52 percent) who are pregnant or parenting in the Let Her Learn Survey reported that not having access to childcare was a barrier to going to school.
- More than three in four girls (76 percent) who are pregnant or parenting stated that schools would do better for them if they provided childcare.

One student mother in the Let Her Learn Focus Groups explained that she wants to "have certainty that I can take my kid to school" and "know that she is close by" so she could respond quickly if an issue were to arise.

Additionally, for many student mothers, the cost of childcare can be prohibitively expensive. The average annual cost of fulltime care for one child can range from $3,000 to over $17,000, depending on the age of the child, the type of care, and where the family lives.

Without assistance, many student mothers are unable to afford childcare. However, whether a student mother will qualify for childcare assistance depends on a variety of factors, including: the state's income eligibility limit, how a state determines a family's income, and whether the income of other family members living with the young parent will be included.

In about half of the states, the size and income of the larger family (including a minor parent's parents and siblings) can be or is required to be considered when determining eligibility. Such eligibility requirements can keep young mothers from receiving childcare assistance and placements, despite the fact that their parents may refuse to help with those expenses. Even when student mothers are eligible for childcare assistance, they may not receive it, or they may be placed on waiting lists for months or years.

A residential academy could provide onsite high-quality childcare where pregnant and parenting students can walk their child to and from class and even interact with them during the day. They can form a secure attachment and learn to prevent ACEs with their child. They could take care of them when they are sick, still remain on campus, and keep up with their academics.

Need for Transportation

A residential academy for pregnant and parenting students and their children would eliminate another barrier pushing pregnant and parenting students out of school: need for transportation. Findings from *Let Her Learn* also revealed a need for transportation (National Women's Law Center, 2017). The study found that even students who have childcare at their schools may not have a way to get their children to those programs. Student parents are often prohibited from taking their children on school buses with them—meaning that they have to find other transportation in order to get both themselves and their children to school. In fact, in some states, it is illegal for children under five to ride on a school bus. Such prohibitions can be particularly challenging for students living in areas with limited public transportation.

Given this context, it is unsurprising that lack of transportation ranked among the top three barriers identified by girls who are pregnant or parenting in the Let Her Learn Survey.

- Girls who are pregnant or parenting (66 percent) were more likely than girls overall (29 percent) to state that not having transportation to and from school made it hard for them to attend.
- Girls who are pregnant and parenting (66 percent) were more likely than girls overall (39 percent) to say that not having a driver's license made it hard for them to go to school.

Quincy faced this educational barrier and was removed from riding the bus when she got to a certain point in her pregnancy. The school did not offer any alternatives for how she could get to school.

> I was riding the bus, so they made me leave school a little earlier. They were afraid that my water would break on the bus. I would say the middle of February is when I was on homebound. And all this time, I'm already nine months pregnant, but all this time, they never knew I was riding the bus, and the thing was, I kept telling myself, "I'm going to go to school until the day I have my child." And I was determined. So, I kept riding the bus to go to school a secret, because they don't want to harm your child—anything like that—if your water breaks, they don't want to put

the bus driver in a bind, and everybody get off hysterical. So I understood where they were coming from. I clearly understood.

A residential academy for pregnant and parenting students and their children would solve this problem of a need for transportation. Students live on campus, which has an onsite daycare that they can walk to on their way to class. It would also solve another educational barrier that is pushing pregnant and parenting students out of school: stress, insufficient time, and the need for work.

Stress, Insufficient Time, and the Need to Work

A residential academy for pregnant and parenting students would eliminate a considerable amount of stress from the need to work and allow them to focus on completing their education and being the best mother that they want to be to their child. According to *Let Her Learn*, in addition to school, girls who are pregnant or parenting have to focus on the day-to-day tasks of raising and caring for a child (National Women's Law Center, 2017). Data reveals that girls who are pregnant or student mothers must also work to support themselves and their children.

This stress can take its toll. The student mothers in the Let Her Learn Focus Groups reported that the need to earn money and care for their children made it hard to succeed in school. According to one student mother, the need to provide for her child was more important than going to school.

Girls who are pregnant or parenting in the Let Her Learn Focus Groups also often felt that they had little control over their lives and had to constantly do things for other people.

- In the Let Her Learn Survey, girls who are pregnant or parenting (53 percent) were even more likely than girls overall (16 percent) to report that having to care for a family member other than their child was a barrier to going to school.

According to one student mother in the focus groups, "You can't have fun because you are so concerned with everything else that is going on in your life." This young woman also said she has to worry about childcare and money.

Again, a residential academy would be a place where pregnant and parenting students can call home for four to five years. They would not have to worry about finances. They would not have to worry about splitting their time between work and being a mom. They could be a student on campus and take care of their child, who lives right there with them. They would have the emotional support of their peers who can identify with their struggle. They could help each other with day-to-day living and rearing their child.

Economic, Housing, and Family Instability

This residential academy would eliminate another major educational barrier that is pushing pregnant and parenting students out of school: economic, housing, and family instability. Lack of economic resources and instability in their living and family situations present a significant barrier for girls who are pregnant and parenting (National Women's Law Center, 2017). They may need services such as Medicaid, nutrition assistance, childcare assistance, Temporary Assistance for Needy Families, and access to housing to help them and their children succeed. For example, pregnant or parenting girls in the Let Her Learn Focus Groups said that having free food at school would help them.

- According to the Let Her Learn Survey, nearly seven in ten (69 percent) pregnant or parenting girls reported that running out of money for necessities like food was a barrier that kept them from being able to go to school.

Unfortunately, complicated rules and requirements may keep girls who are pregnant and parenting from receiving the help they need. For example, the Women, Infants, and Children (WIC) programs provides nutrition assistance to women, infants, and children. However, there is an income limit to receiving assistance, and some girls may not be able to access WIC if they are residing at home and their household income exceeds the threshold, even if the parents or guardians of the pregnant or parenting girl in the household may not be paying for the cost of caring for the infant or child.

In addition, girls who are pregnant or parenting may not have access to affordable housing and may not be able to get placements at homeless shelters. This is particularly concerning given that in the Let Her Learn Survey, girls who were pregnant or parenting were more likely than girls overall to report instability in their living and housing situations.

- Girls who were pregnant or parenting (75 percent) were less likely than girls overall (92 percent) to report that they lived with their parents.
- Girls who were pregnant or parenting (41 percent) were more likely than girls overall (11 percent) to report that they have been homeless, lived with another family, or stayed with another family.
- Girls who were pregnant or parenting (51 percent) were more likely than girls overall (16 percent) to state that not having permanent housing was a barrier to going to school.

A residential academy would eliminate this barrier of not having permanent housing. In the Let Her Learn Survey (National Women's Law Center, 2017), girls who were pregnant or parenting also reported higher rates of instability within their families.

- They were more likely to report that someone in their immediate family had been hurt or injured on purpose by another family member or someone they were dating or going out with (46 percent of girls who were pregnant or parenting compared to 16 percent of girls overall).
- They were more likely to report that someone in their immediate family had been arrested or jailed (51 percent of girls who were pregnant or parenting compared to 25 percent of girls overall).

Another reason for the residential academy for pregnant and parenting students is that, as noted above, pregnant and parenting students, often caught in a cycle of violence, abuse, and teen pregnancy, are living in chaotic households. They must be removed from their environment that is keeping them stuck in co-dependent behaviors, unhealthy boundaries, addictions, and more. This residential academy could be set up to provide

- housing—a major challenge;
- daycare on site—with high quality childcare;
- classes for pregnant and parenting students to earn their high school diploma or GED, or even classes online or at a nearby college or university;
- support-group therapy to help them heal from ACEs and develop healthy interpersonal skills;
- job training classes and opportunities to work from home to earn money to have saved when they leave in four years;
- schooling for their children who have endured ACEs or living with some trauma transferred generationally. This onsite school would employ evidence-based practices to buffer against the challenges they bring with them. They would have a multisensory curriculum. They would have a small class size and looping that allowed students to stay with their teacher for three years.

Realistically, this must happen to make great strides in reducing the 50 percent dropout rate for pregnant and parenting students, to reengage those who have dropped out, and break the intergenerational cycle of abuse, violence, and teen pregnancy. There needs to be a residential academy. A safe place they can call home for several years where they can finish their education and parent their children in a way that breaks the cycle. This would be a huge feat—a huge undertaking—and take significant financial support, but a residential school could make a tremendous impact.

So, in terms of support from home—there is no easy answer, but support from home matters. Graduates were able to finish school because they had a strong female family member from home. For Toni, Diane, Renee and Kelly, that person was their mom. For Quincy, it was her grandmother. So, support from home is needed.

The problem is many pregnant and parenting students don't have a lot of support from home. This is in part why they end up dropping out. So alternative solutions must be considered. Alternative solutions like a surrogate mother figure who can step in, but there are challenges that come with that. Fathers need to take care of their responsibilities. But to really make a dent in the dropout crisis for pregnant and parenting students, to reengage those who have dropped out and to make a significant impact in breaking the intergenerational cycle of violence, abuse, and teen pregnancy (which ultimately leads to poverty), there has to be a residential academy for pregnant and parenting students and their children.

Beyond that, for students who don't have support from home, the support of their teachers, community teen parenting program and faith-based organization are even more important. The next few chapters cover what each can do to help pregnant and parenting students graduate.

NOTES

1. Oprah Winfrey Leadership Academy for Girls—Oprah Winfrey Charitable Foundation (https://www.oprahfoundation.org).

2. Harlem Children's Zone (hcz.org).

3. Oprah Winfrey Leadership Academy for Girls—Oprah Winfrey Charitable Foundation (https://www.oprahfoundation.org).

CHAPTER 4

Support from School Matters

Doctors' appointments, studying, fighting to maintain normalcy as a high school student, developing and maintaining relationships. For pregnant students the weight of responsibilities continues to grow, as does their pregnancy. As noted in the previous chapter, graduates and new moms agree that support from home and their family is integral. They also concur, as you will read in this chapter, that support from the teachers they spend significant time with during the week is an instrumental key to their success.

Xiomara discovered that the engagement, empathy, and concern shown by her ninth-grade English teacher helped her feel less like an outcast.

> When I found out I was pregnant, he was one of the first people I told, even before my daughter's father. He told me like whatever decision I made he supported me. His support continued even when I stopped going to [my home high school]. He still remembers my daughter's birthday.

Laura, like Xiomara, found support in her English teacher— a teacher who came to her emotional rescue when the scorn and judgment of a fellow student was voiced in a classroom setting.

> This guy basically said I wasn't too smart. I was stupid, I got pregnant, or something like that. The English teacher heard it. She said, "Laura, come outside, I need to talk to you." I still don't know how she knew I was really pregnant, but she was like, "You are so smart. You should be a doctor. You can do whatever you want. You are so smart." Just very encouraging words that she said, and asking me, actually, was I in the top ten. I told her the little situation, that I'm not going to be in it or whatever. . . . She cared.

The concern shown by Laura's teacher pushed her to continue to make the highest marks in the class despite typical pregnancy challenges that would arise. Since her teacher habitually read class scores aloud, those who were passing judgment were able to see Laura's continued academic success. At the time of the interview, Laura, a recent graduate from pharmacy school, was a pharmacist for a major retail drug chain.

During her senior year of high school, Toni did not know what her next steps would be. She was the mom of a little boy, with continued aspirations to play women's college basketball. For Toni, a teacher, whom she also considered a mentor, opened her eyes to possibilities. In fact, Toni remembers that the teacher could almost see through her and see the darkness that she was in, as she felt uncertainty about her future.

> So, senior year of high school, now I have a child. What I thought that I was going to do—go play basketball somewhere—everything changed for me at this point because I have a son, who is not even a year old yet. But I also need to get an education so I can support him later on. It was the spring semester of my senior year, and I didn't know where I was going to go to school, or if I was going to school. I did not apply anywhere. At this point I was almost stuck.

But she found out what is true: teachers do more than educate; they inspire, encourage, challenge, and help hopes and dreams seem achievable. Toni knows that sentiment to be true. "Support of teachers was important for me because a lot of them knew me before I got pregnant, so they knew how strong I was before, and they said, "Don't let this stop you." She continued,

> You know, a lot of them (teachers) had their own situations and stories. And that was another thing that some of the teachers shared with me their struggles, with some teachers that I sat there and cried with because the women that they are, you wouldn't know their struggle. Some of them weren't about having a child. It was their own life growing up. I learned from then never let your circumstance determine the outcome. Having supportive, caring teachers was definitely beneficial for me.

Interestingly, Toni's encouraging teacher did not start out that way. Yet, through that teacher's lens of potential, she saw something special in Toni and assured that Toni saw it as well. Toni says,

> We actually didn't get along when we first met. We butted heads; and then somewhere along the line we became very, very close. She was a young, African American woman, who I could relate to, and she kept it real with me. Sometimes, I didn't like what she had to tell me, but it was the truth. Because she knew me, I could always talk to her. So if I left out of the room smiling, that didn't mean that I wasn't crying in the room, because when I found out that I was pregnant she was the first one that I ran to, and I said, "My mom just texted me. I'm probably pregnant."

Toni, her teacher, and several students embarked on a college tour that would crystalize Toni's desire to become a college student.

> On one tour we visited [one university] the same day. The only thing I had heard about these two universities were that they were HBCUs; and that [one university] specifically was a party school. [The university] was a smaller campus. I wasn't feeling it. We went to [a second university]. I absolutely fell in love with the school that day. It was in [a city], an hour and fifteen minutes away from home.
>
> I asked what I needed to do to apply. I got the information then and while we were there, I was calling my mom back and forth, like, "Mom I need this information, this, this, this to see about applying to the school. Even at that point, my teacher was like, "Well, what do you want to do? This is when you decide who you're going to be for the rest of your life. Are you going to let being a teen mom break you and let the odds beat you, or are you going to go on and be great?"

Toni went on to earn her college degree in four years. At the time of her interview, she was a recent college graduate, living in her own apartment and taking care of her son. Her teacher's support and encouragement helped her make her dream a reality.

> "Support of teachers was important for me, because a lot of them knew me before I got pregnant, so they knew how strong I was before, and they said, 'Don't let this stop you.'"
>
> —Toni, a recent college graduate

Quincy, a parenting student, echoes Toni's thoughts on support from her teacher,

> The thing that I actually liked the most was they (my teachers) didn't treat you like an outsider just because you had a child. They treated you like they treated everyone else. They weren't mean and snobbish to you just because you had a child. Now, if they had those thoughts in their head, I would never know, because they didn't treat me any different.

SUPPORT FROM THE SCHOOL NURSE

Several graduates found support from the school nurse. Diane found support from the nurse when she was afraid to tell her parents she was pregnant. As for Quincy, even when the nurse had to tell her she could no longer ride the bus, she felt the nurse was nice about it. Kelly went to the nurse for guidance and that helped her. When asked what some of the things were in school that helped her, as a teen mother, Kelly responded:

> The nurse's office. It really helped me a lot. Just because you can just go to the nurse and just talk to the nurse about being a teen mom, or just to have little pregnancy tests. There was a couple of times I thought I was pregnant in high school [for the second time].

As evidenced from participants' experiences, teachers played a pivotal role in how they graduated. For Xiomara, Laura, and Toni, their teacher encouraged them, saw their potential, and challenged them to push through a teen pregnancy. The school nurse was a source of support for Diane, Quincy, and Kelly.

Teachers can make a huge impact in helping pregnant and parenting students graduate. They are the first line of contact at school. They see students more than anyone else in the school. They are in the best position to support pregnant and parenting students when they are at school.

For pregnant and parenting students who don't have support from home, the support of teachers (and others like the school nurse) is even more important. They can fill that gap and serve as a surrogate mother. Realistically, teachers may be the pregnant or parenting student's only source of encouragement. Their support matters and can be the lifeline that helps pregnant and parenting students graduate.

WAYS TEACHERS CAN SUPPORT PREGNANT AND PARENTING STUDENTS

There are several ways teachers can support pregnant and parenting students. Taking a trauma-informed approach is one of the most important ways teachers can show support. Taking a trauma-informed approach means teachers *realize* students have experienced trauma. They *recognize* the impact of trauma on body, brains, emotions, and behavior. They *respond* in a way that seeks to *resist retraumatizing*. Then teachers set about intentionally creating an atmosphere that *supports each student*, *demonstrates empathy*, and *teaches resilience*.

Taking a Trauma-Informed Approach

Taking a trauma-informed approach is one of the most important way teachers can support pregnant and parenting students. The U.S. Department of Health and Human Service, Substance Abuse and Mental Health Services Administration (SAMSHA) defines taking a trauma-informed approach, using the "4 R's"—Realize, Recognize, Respond, Resist traumatization (SAMSHA, 2014). This means:

- You *realize* or have an understanding or realization of trauma and what it is.
- You *recognize* the signs of trauma and its impact on body, brain, emotions, and behavior.

- You *respond* by applying the principles of a trauma-informed approach:
  - Safety
  - Trustworthiness and transparency
  - Peer support
  - Collaboration and mutuality
  - Empowerment, voice, and choice
  - Cultural, historical, and gender issues
- Which in turn, seeks to *resist retraumatization*.

This is what taking a trauma-informed approach is all about.

> "A program, organization, or system that is trauma-informed *realizes* the widespread impact of trauma and understands potential paths for recovery; *recognizes* the signs and symptoms of trauma in clients, families, staff, and others involved with the system; and *responds* by fully integrating knowledge about trauma into policies, procedures, and practices, and seeks to actively *resist re-traumatization*."
>
> —Substance Abuse and Mental Health Services Administration's Concept of Trauma and Guidance for a Trauma-Informed Approach

As this relates to teachers taking a trauma-informed approach when relating to pregnant and parenting students, this means they *realize* or understand pregnant and parenting students' collective stories of violence and abuse. Realizing this is the first step to taking a trauma-informed approach when relating to pregnant and parenting students.

Teachers taking a trauma-informed approach when relating to pregnant and parenting students means they recognize the signs of trauma (noted below). In the case of pregnant and parenting students, teachers will also want to look for physical signs of interpersonal violence (including intimate partner violence or domestic violence).

Taking a trauma-informed approach means that teachers will *respond* in a way that includes the key principles of a trauma-informed approach such as safety, trustworthiness and transparency and the other key principles. The last R in taking a trauma-informed approach is for teachers to respond to pregnant and parenting students in a way that seek to *resist traumatization.*

Definition and Types of Trauma

Resilient Educator offers a definition for trauma and the different types of trauma. Trauma occurs when a child witnesses or is involved in an event and, as a result, feels intensely threatened. A traumatic event or situation exceeds an individual's ability to cope. Several types of psychological or physical trauma can lead to extreme distress (*Classroom Resources: Trauma Informed Teaching Tips*, n.d.).

One way to consider trauma is as a continuum in frequency and severity, from a single event to multiple events occurring over and over again. The three types of traumas are *acute, chronic,* and *complex.*

1. *Acute trauma* occurs as an isolated event, such as a severe accident, medical procedure, or being a victim of a crime.
2. *Chronic trauma* is when stressful or threatening events are experienced repeatedly, such as domestic violence.
3. *Complex trauma* results from multiple and ongoing traumatic events such as abuse or neglect, living with alcoholism or substance abuse, and suffering from financial, food, and/or housing instability.

Realizing and understanding trauma is the first step to taking a trauma-informed approach when relating to pregnant and parenting students.

> "Child trauma is when a child witnesses or is involved in an event and, as a result, feels intensely threatened. A traumatic event or situation exceeds an individual's ability to cope. Several types of psychological or physical trauma can lead to extreme distress."
>
> —Resilient Educator

Impacts of Trauma

Trauma has both short- and long-term effects on a child's brain and body (*Classroom Resources: Trauma Informed Teaching Tips*, n.d.). Reactions to *acute trauma* may include shaking, crying, or being easily startled. It may be easier to see and understand a child's response to an acute traumatic event because it happens immediately, and one can grasp the reason why the child is distressed.

Chronic and complex trauma can be more challenging to detect in the classroom. A child may appear to be reacting to the situation at hand, but in reality the reaction has been triggered by something else.

Trauma can affect the body and brain in the following ways (*Classroom Resources: Trauma Informed Teaching Tips*, n.d.):

- *Body development*: Trauma can lead to living in a near-constant state of extreme stress or fear. This heightened stress response means the child or adolescent can seemingly overreact emotionally, behaviorally, and/or physically to something that another child may not consider stressful. Children who have been traumatized may also over-respond to stimuli and be extremely sensitive to light and sounds.
- *Brain development*: Trauma often leads to difficulties with language, communication, and processing new information. Reasoning skills are often delayed because of trauma as well.
- *Emotions*: Emotional struggles are common with a trauma history. Children or teens may have difficulties expressing and managing their emotions, quickly exploding and struggling to calm down once upset.
- *Behavior*: Trauma affects the ability to develop healthy attachments and relationships. Distrust, manipulation, argumentative behavior, and impulsivity can be common in youth who have been traumatized.

Become Trauma Informed

The first step for taking a trauma-informed approach is to become trauma informed. Resilient Educator notes that being trauma informed means that one has a level of understanding about trauma and its impacts on an individual's brain, body, emotions, and behavior (as noted above). Being trauma informed is also a commitment to learning more about trauma and viewing the individual as a person and not focusing on their behavior.

Without being trauma informed, a teacher may misinterpret a child's or teen's behavior in the classroom. Being trauma-informed recognizes that the undesirable behaviors are attempts to soothe emotional dysregulation, and this is often done unconsciously on the part of the trauma-impacted individual. It shifts the question from *"What is wrong with this child?"* to *"What has happened to this child?"* (*Classroom Resources: Trauma Informed Teaching Tips*, n.d.).

Having a Trauma-Informed Lens

A trauma-informed lens is a perspective of how the teacher views the child and the classroom. With a trauma-informed lens, a teacher can consider alternatives as to why a student might be acting in a certain way, and can respond in a way that will not cause additional trauma to the child.

Guiding Principles of a Trauma-Informed Approach

Taking a trauma-informed approach means following the six guiding principles of a trauma-informed approach (SAMHSA, 2014):

1. *Safety*: Throughout the school and in each classroom, all people (administration, staff, and students) need to feel physically and psychologically safe.
2. *Trustworthiness and transparency*: Decisions are made and implemented with the primary goal of building and maintaining trust between administration, staff, students, and their families.
3. *Peer support and mutual self-help*: An atmosphere of support is key to building trust and empowerment and in establishing safety.
4. *Collaboration and mutuality*: Everyone—administration, staff, and teachers—has an essential role in developing a trauma-sensitive school. This responsibility is not just for those in thera-

peutic positions; instead, everyone must do the work to create a trauma-informed school.
5. *Empowerment, voice, and choice*: Everyone in the school strives to empower others and recognizes that each student is unique, and both require and deserve an individualized approach. For example, when emotionally dysregulated, a student may be asked what they need to feel better. Providing the student an opportunity to use their voice and select what they want or need empowers the child or teen to recognize what they need, express those needs, and feel calm and heard when those needs are met.
6. *Cultural, historical, and gender issues*: Ignoring stereotypes and biases and ensuring that both teaching and other interactions with students and staff are culturally sensitive and responsive is a crucial part of trauma-informed schools.

Resilient Educator notes that these elements of a trauma-informed approach are not merely a one-time task to be checked off a list. Instead, a true trauma-informed approach is a series of ongoing, deliberate interactions that put the child as an individual at the forefront and not the exhibited behavior (*Classroom Resources: Trauma Informed Teaching Tips*, n.d.).

Trauma-Informed Strategies to Use in Your Classroom

Teachers can take a trauma-informed approach by using the following trauma-informed strategies in the classroom (*Classroom Resources: Trauma Informed Strategies*, n.d.):

1. *Look beyond the behavior*—Research has shown that traumatic experiences alter the brain and can affect children socially, emotionally, behaviorally, and academically—think of all adverse childhood experiences (ACEs) pregnant and parenting students have endured. One trauma-informed strategy is to look beyond the behavior. Instead of jumping to conclusions about the behavior, ask yourself, "What happened to her and why is she behaving this way?"

2. *Build relationships*—Teachers already know how important it is to have good relationships with their students. For pregnant or parenting students affected by ACEs, strong connections are vital. This is why demonstrating empathy is so important. If fuels connection, and that builds relationships. Building relationships is a key factor in teaching resilience, which will be discussed later in this chapter as another way teachers can support students.
3. *Create a safe environment*—Teachers set the tone in their classroom. They play a critical role in making sure students feel safe in their classroom. Students must feel secure in order to learn.
4. *Meet students where they are*—For pregnant or parenting students who have to now manage completing schoolwork, being a new mom, and possibly working at a part-time job, teachers can meet them where they are and make accommodations as they keep up with assignments.
5. *Be predictable*—Feeling out of control is one of the hallmarks of traumatic experiences. Adhering to a clear, predictable routine in your classroom provides students a sense of stability. Stability is what pregnant and parenting students need, as they may be living in a chaotic home environment.

Trauma-Informed Best Practices in the Classroom

Studies have shown that educators can implement several best practices to maximize the support that students who have endured trauma need. Resilient Educator offers these evidence-based trauma interventions (*Classroom Resources: Trauma Informed Teaching Tips*, n.d.).

Recognize the Signs of Trauma

Recognizing the signs of trauma is one best practice to maximize support for students who have endured trauma (*Classroom Resources: Trauma Informed Teaching Tips*, n.d.). In the classroom, signs of trauma may include a student having difficulty focusing, struggling with creating and maintaining friendships, being overly tired, and/or having poor self-regulation. Excessive absences, changes in school performance, and withdrawing from activities or others may also be signs that he or she has been affected by trauma.

For pregnant and parenting students, signs of trauma may show up in the mental health challenges they face because of the prevalence of ACEs in their life. Mental health challenges like depression and anxiety—both impact their ability to focus and concentrate. The student may be withdrawn. She may be overly tired and sleep in class or miss a lot of days. Her grades may drop. This is what happened with Diane, and her teacher recognized the sign that something was different. That's what prompted her teacher to have a conversion with her. So teachers taking a trauma-informed approach and recognizing the signs of trauma is one best practice to maximize support to students.

Provide Consistency and Structure

Another best practice to maximize support to students is to provide consistency and structure (*Classroom Resources: Trauma Informed Teaching Tips*, n.d.). Daily schedules should be structured and contain elements of academics, entertainment or play, and physical exercise or movement. Physical movement might bring physical relief for pregnant and parenting students in their second and third trimester.

Also, weaving in aspects of self-regulation skill building such as breathing exercises, mindfulness, and journaling can be quite helpful so that students can learn to develop these skills and implement them on their own as needed.

This could be a very useful coping skill for a pregnant and parenting student who is struggling with life stressors, and possibly depression and anxiety. Weaving self-regulation skill building into the lessons can be a tremendous benefit to her. Providing her the opportunity to develop these in class will equip her when she is stressed at home or even in other classes. She can practice breathing exercises, mindfulness, and journaling to relieve her symptoms.

Providing an overview each day of the schedule and lessons for the day can also reduce anxiety for those students who may become easily distracted, wondering or fearing what might come next. This quick and straightforward task may help return a bit of control to the student.

Teachers for the most part already incorporate this practice in their daily lessons. What might be helpful for a pregnant and parenting student is to provide her with a weekly or even monthly lesson plan and encourage her to use a day planner to keep up with assignments.

These tips also apply to virtual classrooms. Providing consistency and structure can also be accomplished by setting expectations and goals together as a class, defining responsibilities, and regularly checking in with virtual students to see how they are faring.

> "Weaving self-regulation skill building in the lessons can be a tremendous benefit for pregnant or parenting students who are struggling with depression and anxiety."
>
> —Resilient Educator

Utilize Social-Emotional Learning

Utilizing social-emotional learning can also maximize the support students need (*Classroom Resources: Trauma Informed Teaching Tips*, n.d.). Social-emotional learning, also called SEL, is the process through which students develop skills in critical areas. These areas include self-awareness, self-control, social awareness, interpersonal skills such as feeling and demonstrating empathy for others, effective listening and communication, and making responsible decisions. SEL skills are critical for student success in school, life, and future work.

Social-emotional learning can benefit both pregnant and parenting students as well as their classmates. Utilizing SEL, the student can gain an awareness of others judging her and what that's all about. She can gain an awareness of the dynamics of judgment, shame, and empathy. She can develop coping skills to show herself empathy and compassion.

Simultaneously, the pregnant or parenting student's classmates can learn how to demonstrate empathy for a classmate who is dealing with a major change in life. Many of them possibly experienced a major change—a divorce or death of a loved one. Those who have, know the uncertainty and fear that change can bring. The pregnant or parenting classmate is dealing with that fear and uncertainty. They can learn the importance of demonstrating empathy toward her and others.

Teachers can teach SEL skills in various ways, including modeling behavior, using specially designed SEL curriculum materials, and use them in their *classroom management practices*. In addition to specific *counseling activities to teach social-emotional learning*, these skills can often be introduced in the midst of everyday learning:

- When reading a story during class, discuss how characters might think or feel.
- Assigning responsibilities and tasks to each student builds a sense of self-worth.
- Starting the day with an affirmation can set the tone for a positive learning environment as it encourages positive self-talk and promotes a growth mindset.
- Teaching mindfulness activities such as breathing can be done in conjunction with "brain breaks" in between lessons.
- Journal exercises help students identify and express their feelings or opinions, and group discussions can promote healthy and respectful disagreements.
- Social-emotional learning circles help promote community discussions and respectful, reflective listening.

This evidence-based intervention of teaching SEL skills can go a long way in maximizing the support pregnant and parenting students need.

Use Restorative Practices over Zero-Tolerance Policies

Still another best practice to maximize support for students is to use restorative practices over zero-tolerance policies (*Classroom Resources: Trauma Informed Teaching Tips*, n.d.). Trauma-informed programs realize that zero-tolerance policies are ineffective and harmful. Zero-tolerance policies focus on the offense and are rooted in punishment.

The student is punished for committing an infraction with detention, suspension, or expulsion. This removes the student from the classroom environment but does not consider the student as an individual and what might have led to the misbehavior. Zero-tolerance policies dis-

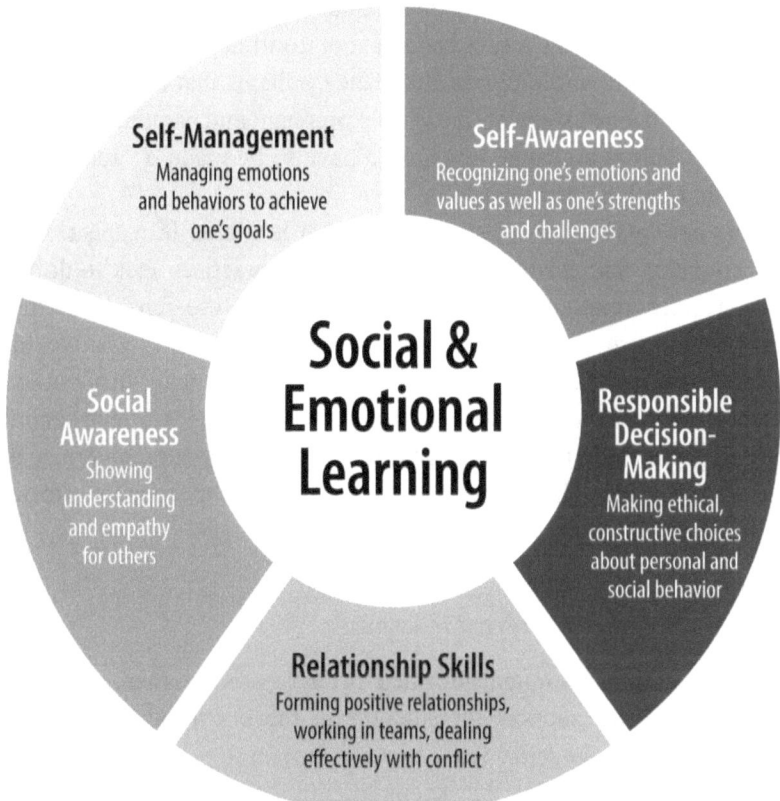

Figure 4.1. Social and Emotional Learning. *CASEL Wheel-Collaborative for Academic, Social, and Emotional Learning.*

proportionately affect students of color, perpetuate the school-to-prison pipeline, and do not provide the support or services the struggling student needs to achieve. Pregnant and parenting students are disproportionately students of color.

Rather than a single technique or tactic, restorative justice is a paradigm shift in how schools consider discipline and how students who break the rules are perceived and addressed. The goal is to create a new disciplinary system that is highly supportive while also being highly controlled.

This is quite relevant to pregnant and parenting students who are often late to school (as in Xiomara's case) or who have absences that are not protected under Title IX. Absences because either they are sick or tired or their child has a fever and cannot go to daycare. A restorative justice approach would create attendance policies that are highly supportive. Such a paradigm shift can help pregnant and parenting students graduate. This is a change that would have to be made by administrators rather than by teachers.

This new restorative disciplinary system is rooted in respect, healing, empathy, and accountability. Restorative practices seek to do just that—restore relationships and environments. Research shows that school-wide use of restorative practices has long-term, positive impacts on student behavior, attendance, and achievement. Dropout and truancy rates decline, and students report being happier while in school. Utilizing this trauma-informed positive behavior support can create an entirely different school environment, especially for students affected by trauma.

Implement a Trauma-Informed Pedagogy

Implementing a trauma-informed pedagogy is another best practice to maximize support for students in the classroom (*Classroom Resources: Trauma Informed Teaching Tips*, n.d.). Trauma-informed pedagogy is the practice that keeps trauma, and how it affects learners, at the forefront when an educator is designing and implementing teaching strategies.

A *trauma-informed pedagogy* also provides content warnings before a teacher discusses potentially triggering topics. Teachers also prepare themselves in advance on how to respond if a student is triggered. A trauma-informed pedagogy allows students to opt out of participating in these discussions and reassures students that they can opt out without any penalties. Trauma-informed pedagogy also describes and teaches grounding techniques for students who may feel overwhelmed. These types of practices help to create a safe and supportive learning environment for all students.

A trauma-informed pedagogy would need to be applied if students are reading a text like *The Scarlet Letter* that may be triggering for an unwed pregnant and parenting student. The teacher can provide content warning about how Hester Prynne, pregnant out of wedlock, has to wear a symbol of shame for the rest of her life. That could be potentially triggering for an unwed pregnant student. The teacher could teach grounding techniques to use if she feels overwhelmed.

These are several best practices that teachers can implement in the classroom to maximize the support that students need:

- Recognize the signs of trauma.
- Provide consistency and structure.
- Utilize social-emotional learning.
- Use restorative practices over zero-tolerance policies.
- Implement a trauma-informed pedagogy.

Using these evidence-based interventions maximizes the support students need to succeed in school.

Teacher Self-Care While Being Trauma-Informed

To create a supportive, trauma-informed classroom, Resilient Educator notes it is imperative that teachers not only identify and deal with their own trauma but also regularly engage in self-care (*Classroom Resources: Trauma Informed Teaching Tips*, n.d.). Self-care techniques can vary based on the teacher's preferences, but examples include exercise, traveling, reading, meditation, yoga, seeing a therapist, and participating in creative or artistic pursuits, such as dancing or painting.

Secondary Traumatic Stress

Resilient Educator also notes that failure to prioritize self-care can lead to burnout or *secondary traumatic stress* (*Classroom Resources: Trauma Informed Teaching Tips*, n.d.). This is significant stress that develops as a result of caring for others with a history of trauma. Hearing about various traumas each day can weigh on a teacher, resulting in both physical and mental difficulties that can severely interfere with one's life.

Warning signs of secondary traumatic stress include:

- Difficulties sleeping/having nightmares
- Excessive fatigue
- Physical aches and pains
- Lack of motivation and/or decreased productivity
- Difficulties concentrating
- Isolation—avoiding people or activities that once brought joy
- Feelings of anxiety, hopelessness, or anger

Secondary traumatic stress is not a permanent condition. Prioritizing self-care, talking to supportive family members, friends, and professionals, and finding healthy outlets to relieve the stress can all help. In time, these difficulties can be resolved, allowing for a clear and healthy mindset ready to support and encourage hurting students.

Professional Development and Training

Resilient Educator stresses that *training is necessary* to develop a trauma-informed classroom (*Classroom Resources: Trauma Informed Teaching Tips*, n.d.). Professional development training is a perfect opportunity to learn about trauma and examine ways to build a supportive environment and trauma-informed communication skills.

Trauma-Informed Professional Development and Training Topics

Trauma-informed training for teachers can include a variety of topics surrounding trauma, including:

- The different types of trauma
- How trauma affects a child's development
- Ways trauma can manifest in students' actions in the classroom
- How and how not to respond to undesirable behaviors
- Developing a trauma-sensitive classroom
- Developing a trauma-informed lens and teaching pedagogy
- School-wide techniques and programs that can be implemented to be responsive to both student and staff stress and trauma

For those who want to become even more well versed in recognizing and managing trauma-based challenging behaviors in the classroom, Resilient Educator notes that options exist for both postgraduate certificates and even a degree in trauma-informed teaching. Spending time learning as much as possible about trauma and how to best support traumatized children in the classroom can have positive and lasting results on both students and the educator.

Taking a trauma-informed approach is vital to the success of pregnant and parenting students. This is one of the most important ways teachers can support students—take a trauma-informed approach. Realize what trauma is, recognized its impact, then respond in a way that seeks to resist retraumitaztion. Then teachers can set about intentionally creating an atmosphere that supports each student, *demonstrates empathy*, and *teaches resilience*.

Demonstrating Empathy

The importance of demonstrating empathy has been emphasized throughout this book. It's the antidote to shame. It fuels connection. If teachers take a trauma-informed approach and then demonstrate empathy toward pregnant and parenting students, they can create a strong emotional connection with their pregnant or parenting student. The student will trust her and the teacher can be an advocate for her.

Brene Brown, in her *Brene Brown on Empathy* (2013) YouTube video paints a clear picture, with a simple illustration, of empathy and how it fuels connection (what pregnant and parenting students need). She notes:

> When someone is in a deep hole and they shout out from the bottom and say, "I'm stuck; It's dark; I'm overwhelmed," and then we look and say Hey, (climb down) I know what it looks like down here and you're not alone. (*Brene Brown on Empathy*, 2013)

That is demonstrating empathy: connecting with the person who is hurting. You connect because you know what it's like to hurt. You may not have experienced that situation—in this case a teen pregnancy—but you know what it feels like to be stuck, in a dark place, and overwhelmed. That is how many pregnant and parenting students feel, and they just need someone to come alongside and say, "I know what it looks like down here and you're not along." That's demonstrating empathy.

Pregnant and parenting students need teachers to demonstrate empathy because they are indeed in a dark place about their teen pregnancy. Toni spoke of the darkness she was in. Diane spoke of feeling stuck. None of the graduates interviewed for this project who experienced teen pregnancy were happy about being pregnant. They were disappointed in themselves and their families, but what can you do once you're pregnant?

One graduate, Toni, was disappointed when she found out she was pregnant, but she had to accept it:

> I was a teen mom, so even if I didn't want that to show on the outside that I was struggling, it was a struggle for me. A disappointment in myself, but this is my reality, this is what I'm going to have to do at this point. Everything that I was or wanted to be had changed at this point, so everything went smoothly, but inside, I didn't know what the next step was for me. I didn't know how my college experience was going to be. I just hoped for the best, and I had so much support even if I wanted to crawl up in a ball, I couldn't.

That is what all pregnant and parenting students need: "so much support even if they wanted to crawl in a ball, they wouldn't be able to." A part of this support comes from their teachers. After taking a trauma-informed approach and demonstrating empathy, teachers can focus on helping students build resilience. Building resilience will help them graduate.

Build Resilience

In combination with taking a trauma-informed approach and demonstrating empathy, teachers can support pregnant and parenting students by helping them build resilience. Resilience is the ability to bounce back from adversity. Teachers play an essential role in helping students develop this determination and ability to bounce back—to persevere through difficult times.

In an article in Edutopia, "5 Ways to Build Resilience in Students," the following points are noted (Gonser, 2021):

- When educators help students "cultivate an approach to life that views obstacles as a critical part of success, we help them develop resilience," *writes Marilyn Price-Mitchell, a developmental psychologist and author.*
- "Resilience is not a genetic trait. It is derived from the ways that children learn to think and act when faced with obstacles large and small."
- When the adults in children's lives—caregivers, teachers, coaches—help young people develop resilience, it helps them "emerge from challenging experiences with a positive sense of themselves and their futures," says Price-Mitchell.
- It's a skill that takes practice. "Resilience works like a muscle we can build through effort and repetition, and we want to keep our muscles strong and flexible so we can think of many ways to solve a problem," so says Mary Alvord, a psychologist and author.
- "At the core, resilience is the belief that while you can't control everything in your life, there are many aspects you can control, including your attitude."

Pregnant and parenting students need resilience if they are to succeed. They need to note what an unknown pregnant and parenting student expressed: "Teen pregnancy should not be worn as a badge of honor; but neither is it a death sentence. You can recover." Proof of this are the graduates in the book.

Five Ways to Build Resilience

Building resilience gives students the tools they need to deal with adversity, and Edutopia offers five ways to build resilience (Gonser, 2021).

Set Brave Goals

A big part of developing resilience involves being able to identify personal goals, and then being able to tolerate the discomfort that's creating resistance toward that goal. With pregnant and parenting students, their journey into parenthood brings questions and doubts. Teachers can assure pregnant and parenting students that if they can "tolerate the discomfort" and push forward, their graduating from high school will be a sweet success. Teachers can encourage them through the stories of Quincy, Toni, Renee, Xiomara, and other students like them that academic success remains possible, as do prosperous and productive lives outside of school.

Quincy speaks proudly of a goal she set and what others doubted.

> I feel successful. I feel great. I feel like I did something that a lot of parents don't do, and it makes me feel good. And it makes you look good. It makes you look wonderful because people get so excited when you tell them that you graduated from high school as a teenage parent. So, it makes you feel good. Leaves you speechless. I feel like I accomplished something. I had people tell me I would never do it. And now I'm looking back at them like, "Ha. I told you so." So, I mean, it makes you feel good. And it means a lot to me.

Toni, who succeeded through high school and became a college graduate, shares Quincy's exuberance about her achievements.

> It [graduating from college] definitely means a lot. And so, when I say that I have a child—you know some people—because they'll ask, "How old's your son?" And when I say, "Six." They go, "Well, how old are you?" I say, "Well, Twenty-four." So, you do the math in your head, and it's not anything daunting for me because I still did everything I was supposed to do. I still went to school, and I was able to finish school on time. I did what I had to do. Now I'm taking care of what I have to do. If not, I would feel some kind of way if I knew that I was struggling or knew that I hadn't properly prepared myself to care for him, but there's no shame here.

Renee, currently in college, is looking forward to the day that she can tell her daughter about her success in the face of challenges and negativity. "It [graduating from high school] means a lot to me because when my daughter gets older, I want to be able to tell her, 'No matter what, I made it. I graduated on time. I didn't let pregnancy stop me. It motivated me.'"

Xiomara not only nailed graduating from high school, but revels in her new role as a college student.

> It [going to college] means that my daughter can have a great future, you know? I feel like I wasn't there, and her life starting out the way it did, I'm going to make it right, eventually. When I graduate from college and have a career, I will be able to not only support her but give her everything that she wants, not just everything that she needs.

Teachers can remind pregnant and parenting students of the sense of accomplishment they will feel if they go ahead—push through the adversity—and graduate. Encouraging pregnant and parenting to set brave goals will help them build resilience.

Remind Them to Do It for Their Child

Teachers can also help pregnant and parenting students build resilience by reminding them how graduating will benefit their child. Those who have a loving, nurturing relationship with their pregnant and parenting student(s), can show how impactful their choices will be in the nurturing of their children.

Quincy, who says she was not a party girl or wild child in high school, found that becoming a teenage mom made her look forward to doing things. "It made me want to be successful because now it wasn't just me living my life for me. It was me living my life for me and my child."

Like Quincy, Renee set her resolve to succeed despite pregnancy in her teen years and becoming a mom so young. Renee says no one around thought she was going to succeed at graduating while being a mom.

> A lot of people thought I wasn't going to do it because, "Oh, she got pregnant, you know. She's playing around in school." But actually, when I got pregnant, that's when I took high school more seriously. After I got

pregnant, with my little girl, I took my high school classes—I took them seriously because I felt like, I'm about to have a baby and I want her to know no matter what you go through, you can still make it.

When Renee graduated in 2010 with her class, she shed tears of joy, not only because her mom was there, but so was someone else incredibly special to her. "My little girl was there, watching me get my diploma from high school. So, yeah, I cried. Momma was happy."

If teachers can show pregnant and parenting students how impactful their choices will be in the nurturing of their child, that will help them build resilience. That will motivate them—just like Quincy and Renee—to push through the adversity.

Model Learning from Mistakes

Learning from failure is paramount to becoming a resilient pregnant or parenting student. Teachers can help by creating a classroom where "failure, setbacks, and disappointment are an expected and honored part of learning," where students are "praised for their hard work, perseverance, and grit, not just for grades and easy successes," and where they are held accountable for producing work about which they feel "ownership and internal reward."

Teachers can create a classroom bulletin board where, in addition to showcasing students' achievements, "students can brag about their biggest mistakes and what they learned from them." It is helpful if teachers tell the class about their own mistakes, especially if they are funny, and what you learned from them. Give students opportunities to correct mistakes and resubmit work and be sure to recognize when their work improves because nothing shows learning from mistakes more than improvement.

Teachers can also explicitly label some activities "rough-draft thinking" giving students permission to ask questions, make mistakes, and then revise without the stifling prospect of failure.

Encourage Responsible Risks

Teachers can help pregnant and parenting students build resilience by encouraging responsible risks. Edutopia notes that resilience has been compared to a stress ball. A stress ball is resilient because it springs back to its original shape after being squeezed. Likewise, when students experience stress or frustration, they can think of that as pressure on them that they need to spring back from. The hope in presenting them with strategies to build resilience is that those strategies will ease the frustration and help them get back into optimal and productive focus for learning.

One way to foster resilience is to recognize and compliment students when they take responsible risks and challenge themselves—even and maybe especially when they don't achieve the desired results. For example, speaking up to answer a question during class, even if the answer is incorrect, or "stumbling on words while reading out loud." "These are opportunities to build confidence, and risk-taking, and most importantly, to keep a resilient momentum going forward while in a safe space."

Label Difficult Emotions

Teachers can also help pregnant and parenting students build resilience by helping them label difficult emotions. Recognizing and naming emotions can help students become self-aware and begin to manage their own emotional states effectively—psychologists call this labeling. Once students learn to notice, name, and interpret their emotions, they are better prepared to make rational decisions and manage disorienting or disruptive emotions in their lives—critical elements of resilience. For pregnant and parenting students this could mean teachers help them recognize and name difficult emotions like guilt, shame, feeling judged, and feeling unwanted in the school building. Helping them notice, name, and interpret their emotions is a critical element in showing them how to build resilience.

Write and Talk about Setbacks and Human Resilience

Writing assignments that focus on "sources of personal strength" can help pregnant and parenting students explore different ways to build resilience. A few prompts to get started include: "Write about a person who supported you during a particularly stressful or traumatic time.

How did they help you overcome this challenge? What did you learn about yourself?"

Another idea: "Write about a time in your life when you had to cope with a difficult situation. What helped and hindered you as you overcame this challenge? What learning did you take away that will help you in the future?"

The topic of resilience isn't bound to one class—ELA, for example—it's relevant across the curriculum. Opportunities abound to connect resilience with personal success. A starting point is to expand discussions about political leaders, scientists, literary figures, innovators, and inventors beyond what they accomplished to the personal strengths they possess, and the hardships they endured and overcame to reach their goals. Teachers can help students learn to see themselves and their own strengths through these success stories.

Summary

Support from teachers matters. Teachers are the first line of contact at school. They see students more than anyone else in the school. Several graduates echoed the sentiments the support of their teachers helped them graduate. Teacher can help current pregnant and parenting students by taking a trauma-informed approach. Taking a trauma-informed approach means they realize or have an understanding of trauma and what it is; recognized its impact on body, brain, emotions, and behavior; then respond in a way that seeks to resist retraumatization. Ways teachers can resist retraumatization include using trauma-informed strategies and trauma-informed best practices in the classroom. After taking a trauma-informed approach, teachers can help pregnant and parenting students graduate by demonstrating empathy and helping them build resilience. Support from teachers matters.

CHAPTER 5

Support from the Community Matters

The old TV show *Amen* aired an episode (November 1986) where the lead pastor advises a pregnant teenage girl who was a faithful member of the choir that she can no longer sing with them because of her condition. The episode turned the spotlight onto how an integral community partner, in this case the church, can turn its back on pregnant teenage moms, but support from the community matters. In this chapter, you will also hear from graduates about how community teen parenting programs helped them graduate. You will read how, for some graduates, they found support from their church. You will learn about several programs designed to support pregnant and parenting students.

On the ring of pertinent keys to success for pregnant and parenting students is support from the community, specifically teen parenting programs. Whether these programs are offered in schools, through organizations, or through religious entities, students have found the resources made available to be vital to them and their unborn or new baby. These programs are most often tailored with the unique needs of pregnant and parenting students in mind and staffed compassionately so that their emotional and mental needs are also served.

The U.S. Department of Education, Office for Civil Rights (OCR) in their pamphlet *Supporting the Academic Success of Pregnant and Parenting Students* provides an overview of programs designed to support pregnant and parenting student (*Supporting the Academic Success of Pregnant and Parenting Students*, 2013). They note that while not required by Title IX, some school districts have established programs to help pregnant and parenting students stay in school, graduate, and acquire the skills needed for parenting. (*Supporting the Academic Success of Pregnant and Parenting Students*, 2013). In the absence of these programs, school can provide leadership in coordinating the education, health care, counseling, and childcare needed by pregnant and parenting students.

These programs can provide these students with peer support and encouragement to help prevent the feelings of isolation that they may experience. They can reduce the dropout rate, provide comprehensive prenatal care, and improve the health of student parents and their children.

To provide schools with information, the OCR describes the programs that can supplement pregnant and parenting students' regular academic course work (*Supporting the Academic Success of Pregnant and Parenting Students*, 2013). The list of programs is not exhaustive and may not be applicable to every specific setting in a particular school. The list and overview of programs is provided only as examples and is not legally mandated by Title IX. Below are descriptions of each program. Alongside each, graduates share how those programs helped them graduate.

PROGRAMS DESIGNED TO SUPPORT PREGNANT AND PARENTING STUDENTS

Prenatal, Parenting, and Life Skills Programs

Prenatal, parenting, and life skills programs can provide pregnant and parenting students' the much-needed support and resources they need to graduate. Pregnant and parenting students may need prenatal programs to learn about nutrition, exercise, and caring for themselves while pregnant.

Some schools have developed courses for credit, special classes during free periods, and after-school prenatal care programs. Schools can assist students in accessing such programs provided by other entities, such as community-based nonprofits, and can even offer course credits to students who take part in such programs.

Prenatal care programs may include not only pregnant students but also their partners, who can give invaluable support during pregnancy and after birth. Other programs may provide information and training in parenting skills and child development, including courses in child health and infant stimulation.

Some of these programs include school nurseries, where students gain practical experience diapering, feeding, and bathing infants. Schools may also provide life-skills courses to teach pregnant and parenting students (both young men and young women) lessons on time management, including balancing schoolwork and parenting, and handling finances, so that they can continue and complete school.

These programs also help prepare pregnant and parenting students for the challenges posed by higher education and work, such as by providing job-readiness training and mentoring services. They also may facilitate access for pregnant and parenting students to many health and social service programs.

Graduates' Experiences

Several graduates participated in community-based teen parenting programs or parenting classes. These programs and classes were crucial in helping students graduate. Faith-based organization and reliance on their faith was also a source of support and helped them graduate.

Xiomara expressed her gratitude, acknowledging that she could not have graduated without the support of her teen parenting program:

Oh, [my teen parenting program] was the greatest program that ever existed. [They] help you to stay in school by any means necessary. When I say, "By any means necessary"—

No, that's not their motto, but that's what they do. It's their not nonprofit organization, and when I say, "By any means necessary," that means they paid for my car to get repaired. When I was going through a few months and I didn't have a job, they let me come file papers in their office and paid me ten dollars an hour. When something happened with my financial aid, they paid my tuition when I was in college. They gave me a laptop—a new laptop—because I had the highest GPA in the program.

They did every—Christmas rolls around, they give you gift cards to go Christmas shopping. They have meetings every week where they'll come get you. They'll send like a Lincoln Towncar to come get you and your child and bring you to this meeting. At the meeting, they have childcare so you don't have to be bothered with your child, and it's like an informational meeting—all different types of stuff like budgeting, how to finance, going to college—like just so much stuff. When my daycare got cut off, they paid for her to go to daycare. They're going to keep you in school. They don't care what they have to do. By any means necessary.

For Xiomara, her teen parenting class was "most definitely" supportive in helping her finish school and stay in college. Xiomara also provided an overview of how her program worked:

You have to keep your GPA up. Your GPA drops below—I don't know if it's a 3.0 or a 2.5—and that disqualifies you. You have to be in high school and be a teenage mother.

And you have to actually be going to high school, or you have to be working if you just graduated high school, so they definitely have—they have like, high qualifications to be in their program, but they help you so much that they should.

Toni, a recent college graduate, reflecting on what would have helped her with her internal struggles, said she had the support she needed to graduate. Support from home, from her teachers, but specifically, the teen parenting program she was a part of:

I think I did have that help, and that's how I was able to keep going. I don't think that anybody's going to wake up and say, "Oh it's fine!" You're going to have that within yourself, when there's a life-altering situation going on. You now have a child. Regardless of what kind of help, you're going to have your own internal things that you deal with on a day-to-day.

Even somebody that doesn't have a child, they're still dealing with their own situations. So the support that I had was necessary for me between the family support, the support at school, the programs that are geared specifically toward teenage mothers—the support that I would've needed, I had.

Reflecting, Toni readily admits that her teen parenting program specifically played a major role in helping her graduate:

The adolescent parenting programs specifically—because everyone in the room is just like you. Now you no longer feel alone. You no longer are wondering, by yourself, how you're going to do it because they would often bring other girls who were like two steps ahead. When you see somebody that's just like you, that played basketball just like you, that was very popular just like you, and now they have a child, and now they're in college, and now they're about to graduate. You say, "Well, if she can do it, why can't I?" Why would I crawl up and say, "Now I can't do it?" Because I'm looking at somebody that has, and that is, and that will.

For Quincy, her teen parenting classes helped her graduate, and she was able to support those pregnant and parenting students coming after her.

I took parenting classes. The daycare he (my son) went to provided it. I was in parenting classes for my tenth through twelfth grade year. As time progressed, we had new teen parents, and they were new to this, and so I would share my experience with them, and I would help them with situations that they were in because I had already been in it. And I would give them advice about what was—like what was going on with them—I would give them advice, or they would ask you sometimes, "Quincy, how do you do it?"

For Renee, teen parenting classes not only helped her with resources and information but gave the encouragement to seek a college education. She spoke of how the first time she thought about going to college was when leaders in her teen parenting class brought it up.

The class wasn't required, but they just feel that teen mothers should go to the classes, and it helps them to talk about their pregnancy, what they're going through, and they help you talk about college. Want you to get into it, and that's when I started thinking about college, when they was telling me about it.

There was one [parenting class] that's offered toward the morning, or you could pick one after school. A group of girls come in and give us some snacks. We just talk about what we're going through, what we're facing while we're in high school, and where do we plan to go when we get out of high school, and when they said, "College would be a great start," and, "There's not a lot of single mothers that's in college, but I believe y'all can do it." And they talked about the future of our child. That's when I decided, "I think I'm going to go to college."

It [participating in the parenting class] was helpful because it also—they said that "If you stay in school, they keep helping you." So, it makes it seem like, "Okay, if I go to school, I'll still have the help."

They'll help you with if your baby needs Pampers. If you need a daycare, they'll help your child be in daycare as long as you was in school. They was helping, and I thought like that's a push right there for girls to keep going on in college and stuff.

Kelly elaborated on how here teen pregnancy program worked—"You had to keep your grades up and be on birth control and show proof of birth control each month." When asked how she felt about that, she thought it was a great idea!

It's perfect. I think if people have programs like that—well, everybody's different. Some places may have programs where they're supporting the teen mothers and stuff and not asking them to be on birth control, but I think it's a very smart thing, because obviously, if you're having sex, there's a possibility you can get pregnant. If your main goal is to prevent them from having another pregnancy, you should definitely have them on birth control.

Time Management Skills

One area of development for teen parenting programs to include that Xiomara and Alger spoke of is to teach time management skills. Knowing how to manage their time would have been a helpful class or workshop for them. Xiomara talked about this struggle.

Time management, mostly. Just trying to—like just the balance of having a full-time job, having a child, and going to school full-time and not wanting to burden anybody with [her daughter] all the time. Just that type of struggle, and not having time to study, and having to sacrifice like, "Do I want to study tonight, or do I want to go to sleep? Do I want to go to class today, or do I want to go to work? Because they want me to work."

Alger spoke of her struggle:

> It's definitely time management and it's also just putting your best foot forward on your worst day. I think that's the main thing, time management and just being able to—because when you're raising a child, you want to be able to teach them and spend time with them, just be the best mother. That is a huge struggle for me.

Need for Continued Funding

A topic of concern that was brought up was continued funding for teen parenting programs. Toni addressed how some lawmakers are seeking to reduce funding for teen parenting programs that provide childcare. She addressed this issue of continued funding to teen parenting programs in an interview. She was advocating because even though the teen pregnancy rates are steadily declining, girls are still getting pregnant, and they need the support of teen parenting programs.

> These same programs that I was a part of. If the school itself can't have the programming, at least seek the resources for the teenage mothers to get to those programs that are available, as well as advocation for the necessity of the program, because some state officials feel like—because they were saying that the teenage pregnancy rate was dropping in [my state].

> But that's on the preventative side. There are still people—still females—that are becoming pregnant, and those are the ones that we have to focus on. So even if the statistics are dropping for preventative measures, we still need to focus on the females that are becoming pregnant, and ensure that they have the support that they would need because if I didn't have [my teen parenting program], I don't know how my situation would have turned out, and that's through—because your mother, she's there. She's going to support you.

> But identifying who I am and having that support system of other females who are just like me, as well as targeted parenting skills to understand exactly what we're supposed to do, why is my child doing this, is he supposed to be here, is he not supposed to be here, as well as the support and encouragement to go on to go to college. That was their

main goal. That's their mission. That's all that they do. So, without that, I don't know where I would be, if my situation would have turned out as well as it did.

Continued Areas of Improvement

Based on the experiences of graduates and the results of the Let Her Learn Focus Group Study, one area of growth and continued improvement for teen parenting programs is to address crucial topics that relate to pregnant and parenting students. Crucial topics like:

1. Title IX: know your rights
2. Understanding shame
3. Empathy: the antidote to shame
4. Interpersonal violence and teen pregnancy
5. Adverse childhood experiences
6. Children of teen moms
7. The teen pregnancy and birth rate
8. Repeat pregnancy rate for teen parents

Gaining knowledge of these critical topics related to their experiences will help them understand the challenges they are facing and how to overcome them.

Offer Guidance for Going to College

Teen parenting programs can offer additional support to pregnant and parenting students by providing them guidance on going to college. For Renee, the first time she thought about going to college was when one of the leaders in her teen parenting classes mentioned about single moms going to college.

One way teen parenting programs can guide student is in applying for financial aid—like the Pell Grant. Inform them to apply as soon as the application process begins in January. Advise them of the paperwork they will need from their parents. Offer a workshop and guide the students and their parents in applying for financial aid. Renee spoke on how applying for financial aid was hard, and it would have helped if she had guidance.

> Well, in my parenting class, they have college fliers of [first local community college] and [second local community college]. And I wanted to pick somewhere close, so I looked at [first local community college]. I started looking at programs, and I had been on financial aid, which that was a hard process.

> The school had to help me because I had a lot of errors. I didn't know how to fill that out. I know a lot of girls who said that financial aid is the hardest process on getting through college. But still, I went to the school, and I was talking to the advisor, and she was just telling me all the programs and all the classes, and how it will be, the new people you'll meet. So, I just went on from there.

Bring in Admissions Counselors

One way community teen parenting programs can offer guidance for attending college is to bring in admissions counselors from local colleges—*particularly from the community college because many pregnant and parenting students started out at the community college.* Xiomara is one example. She started at the community college and at the time of the interview, she had just received her acceptance letter from the local research university.

> I'm about to graduate from [the local community college]. [With] my Associates in Arts. I've gotten accepted into [the local four-year university], so I'm going to go there for my communications degree.

Laura, too, started out at the local community college. She then transferred to a four-year university and after undergraduate studies, she completed pharmacy school.

Bringing in admissions counselors, especially from the local community college, is a great way to support pregnant and parenting students. Combined with time management skills, counselors will help them manage going to college, working, and being a parent.

Childcare and Early-Learning Programs

Other programs the OCR highlights that are designed to support pregnant and parenting students are childcare and early-learning programs. These programs help keep parenting students in school by offering childcare and early childhood education. They also enhance parenting skills and may provide transportation for students and their children. Even schools that cannot house a childcare center can help pregnant and parenting students locate and secure high-quality, affordable early-learning programs and services and connect parenting students with available resources in the community.

One major educational barrier pregnant and parenting students face is not having childcare, but graduates participated in teen parenting program or class that provided childcare. Their teen parenting programs and classes had onsite childcare, or they had funding to provide vouchers for daycare to parenting students. Renee, Toni, Quincy, and Xiomara spoke of how critical having childcare was in helping them graduate.

Dropout Prevention Programs

The OCR highlights another type of program designed to support pregnant and parenting students: dropout prevention programs. These programs identify students at a higher risk of dropping out, contact them, and encourage them to remain in or return to school. The programs can provide flexible academic options for pregnant and parenting students so that they do not fall too far behind in earning credits toward graduation. They may also include an academic credit recovery component to help students who have already fallen far behind get back on track.

Summary

These are three major types of programs that the OCR highlights that can provide the support pregnant and parenting students need to graduate. As noted earlier, while not required by Title IX, some school districts have established programs to help pregnant and parenting students stay in school, graduate, and acquire the skills needed for parenting. (*Supporting the Academic Success of Pregnant and Parenting Students*, 2013). These programs were crucial for helping graduates finish school. In the absence of these programs, school can provide leadership in coordinating the education, health care, counseling, and childcare pregnant and parenting students need to help them graduate.

Faith Community

For Alger, Kelly, and Xiomara, going to church in their community and their faith offered them emotional support to keep going. Alger spoke of the emotional support she received from her church family:

> I probably couldn't have done it [graduated] if I didn't go to church. It was very, very opening arms to me, just because I didn't feel like people were staring at me. Everyone knew I was young, just because I even did some of the choir members' hair, so everybody knew my age, so when I walked in and pregnant, they already knew. I felt like I wasn't judged, and I was just welcomed with open arms.

For Kelly too—her faith in God made the difference as did being part of the community-based teen parenting program:

> I did it mostly by God, just having faith in Him. I've always been a go-getter, so I'm not going to stop something without completing it. I definitely knew I was going to graduate from high school. My mom, my dad, nobody's ever had to be like, "Make good grades."
>
> I've never been the bad child. I just happened to have a child, so God, [my teen parenting program coordinator], the whole [teen parenting program] people, [the program director], they helped me. They made it so your grades have to be up. If your grades aren't up, you're kicked out of the program, your child's not getting daycare, stuff like that.
>
> I applied to be in their college program, the [program], because I was in the [other] program as well, when I was in high school with them, and that's for the teenage mothers that are in [teen parenting program], but they're like the leaders, so I was in that program. Then I applied to be in the [other program], that's a step up from high school to college, and

it's the teen mothers still. They helped me get a laptop, a laptop bag and stuff. They really helped me, and even now, they fund me with some money each semester for school.

Kelly's grandmother's church took a big leap of faith in assuring her educational success, providing a much-needed scholarship.

My grandmother always told me her church always has little awards or little scholarships. They're only a hundred dollars or so, but that's still more than what I had when I came up in there, so I always write the little essays, read them, and hope I win.

Laura found that community programs, like Kelly's grandmother's church, could be a great resource for college scholarship information.

There's a lot of scholarships that you get for being a parent that you wouldn't get if you didn't have a child. That in itself, that actually helped me out a lot. I got the Pell Grant. That helped a lot, and then I had an honors scholarship that's based on your grades, The [name of] Scholarship. That helped out.

I got that all through undergrad, except for my last semester I didn't get it, because I had taken too many hours, so I couldn't get it, but I did get the Pell grant the entire time. That helped quite a bit as well.

That's provided to, I believe, anyone who has dependents. I got a scholarship just from what I was majoring in—a women in science and engineering scholarship. There are a lot of scholarships out there that can help, if you think that finances are going to be a problem, and even just the finances alone, I feel like, as far as undergrad went, I got paid to go to school. I would get my refund check after they paid for all my classes. I would just have to pay for my books, but I would still have money left where I could divide it up to help pay my rent. Say I'm only going to have to pay half of my rent with my money I used to work with, because of grants and scholarships.

Graduates paint a vivid image of how community-based teen parenting programs and faith-based organization can help students graduate not only at the high school level but also at the collegiate level.

Community-Based Support Groups

As noted earlier, each pregnant and parenting student has her own story, but teen moms have a collective story of violence and abuse. The *Interpersonal Violence and Adolescent Pregnancy* report outlines the story of violence and abuse and details how violence, abuse, and teen pregnancy are intertwined (Leiderman and Almo, 2001). The report further notes how critical it is for parents to heal from their own violent experiences to attend to the emotional needs of their children. Healing from their own experiences will help them as well. Two community-based support groups that can help them heal are Co-Dependents Anonymous and Teen Moms Anonymous.

Co-Dependents Anonymous Co-Dependents Anonymous is a twelve-step recovery program designed to help people develop functional, healthy relationships. The only requirement for membership is a desire for a healthy and loving relationships. The Mental Health Alliance[1] provides detailed information on co-dependency, including a definition and responses to the questions below. This information is worth reading for pregnant and parenting students and all those who support them.

- Whom does co-dependency affect?
- What is a dysfunctional family and how does it lead to co-dependency?
- How do co-dependent people behave?
- Characteristics of co-dependent people
- Questionnaire to identify signs of co-dependency
- How is co-dependency treated?
- When co-dependency hits home

Co-Dependency

Co-dependency is a learned behavior that can be passed down from one generation to another. It is an emotional and behavioral condition that affects an individual's ability to have a healthy, mutually satisfying relationship. It is also known as "relationship addiction" because people with co-dependency often form or maintain relationships that are one-sided, emotionally destructive and/or abusive.

The disorder was first identified as the result of years of studying interpersonal relationships in families of alcoholics. Co-dependent behavior is learned by watching and imitating other family members who display this type of behavior.

Whom Does Co-Dependency Affect?

Co-dependency often affects a spouse, a parent, sibling, friend, or coworker of a person afflicted with alcohol or drug dependence. Originally, *co-dependent* was a term used to describe partners in chemical dependency, persons living with, or in a relationship with an addicted person. Similar patterns have been seen in people in relationships with chronically or mentally ill individuals. Today, however, the term has broadened to describe any co-dependent person from any dysfunctional family.

What Is a Dysfunctional Family and How Does It Lead to Co-Dependency?

A dysfunctional family is one in which members suffer from fear, anger, pain, or shame that is *ignored or denied. Underlying problems may include any of the following:*

- An addiction by a family member to drugs, alcohol, relationships, work, food, sex, or gambling
- The existence of physical, emotional, or sexual abuse
- The presence of a family member suffering from a chronic mental or physical illness

Dysfunctional families do not acknowledge that problems exist. They don't talk about them or confront them. As a result, family members learn to repress emotions and disregard their own needs. They become "survivors." They develop behaviors that help them deny, ignore, or avoid difficult emotions. They detach themselves. They don't talk. They don't touch. They don't confront. They don't feel. They don't trust. The identity and emotional development of the members of a dysfunctional family are often inhibited.

Attention and energy focus on the family member who is ill or addicted. The co-dependent person typically sacrifices his or her needs to take care of a person who is sick. When co-dependents place other people's health, welfare and safety before their own, they can lose contact with their own needs, desires, and sense of self. This is often what pregnant and parenting students must do to survive their chaotic and dysfunctional home environments.

> Dysfunctional families do not acknowledge that problems exist. They don't talk about them or confront them. As a result, family members learn to repress emotions and disregard their own needs.
>
> —Mental Health Alliance

How Do Co-Dependent People Behave?

Co-dependents have low self-esteem and look for anything outside of themselves to make them feel better. They find it hard to "be themselves." Some try to feel better through alcohol, drugs, or nicotine—and become addicted. Others may develop compulsive behaviors like workaholism, gambling, or indiscriminate sexual activity.

They have good intentions. They try to take care of a person who is experiencing difficulty, but the caretaking becomes compulsive and defeating. Co-dependents often take on a martyr's role and become "benefactors" to an individual in need. A wife may cover for her alcoholic husband; a mother may make excuses for a truant child; or a father may "pull some strings" to keep his child from suffering the consequences of delinquent behavior.

The problem is that these repeated rescue attempts allow the needy individual to continue on a destructive course and to become even more dependent on the unhealthy caretaking of the "benefactor." As this reliance increases, the co-dependent develops a sense of reward and satisfaction from "being needed." When the caretaking becomes compulsive, the co-dependent feels choiceless and helpless in the relationship, but is unable to break away from the cycle of behavior that causes it. Co-dependents view themselves as victims and are attracted to that same weakness in the love and friendship relationships.

Characteristics of Co-Dependent People

- An exaggerated sense of responsibility for the actions of others
- A tendency to confuse love and pity, with the tendency to "love" people they can pity and rescue
- A tendency to do more than their share, all of the time
- A tendency to become hurt when people don't recognize their efforts
- An unhealthy dependence on relationships. The co-dependent will do anything to hold on to a relationship; to avoid the feeling of abandonment
- An extreme need for approval and recognition
- A sense of guilt when asserting themselves
- A compelling need to control others
- Lack of trust in self and/or others
- Fear of being abandoned or alone
- Difficulty identifying feelings
- Rigidity/difficulty adjusting to change
- Problems with intimacy/boundaries
- Chronic anger
- Lying/dishonesty
- Poor communications
- Difficulty making decisions

Questionnaire to Identify Signs of Co-Dependency

This condition appears to run in different degrees, whereby the intensity of symptoms is on a spectrum of severity, as opposed to an all or nothing scale. Please note that only a qualified professional can make a diagnosis of co-dependency; not everyone experiencing these symptoms suffers from co-dependency.

1. Do you keep quiet to avoid arguments?
2. Are you always worried about others' opinions of you?
3. Have you ever lived with someone with an alcohol or drug problem?
4. Have you ever lived with someone who hits or belittles you?
5. Are the opinions of others more important than your own?

6. Do you have difficulty adjusting to changes at work or home?
7. Do you feel rejected when significant others spend time with friends?
8. Do you doubt your ability to be who you want to be?
9. Are you uncomfortable expressing your true feelings to others?
10. Have you ever felt inadequate?
11. Do you feel like a "bad person" when you make a mistake?
12. Do you have difficulty taking compliments or gifts?
13. Do you feel humiliation when your child or spouse makes a mistake?
14. Do you think people in your life would go downhill without your constant efforts?
15. Do you frequently wish someone could help you get things done?
16. Do you have difficulty talking to people in authority, such as the police or your boss?
17. Are you confused about who you are or where you are going with your life?
18. Do you have trouble saying "no" when asked for help?
19. Do you have trouble asking for help?
20. Do you have so many things going at once that you can't do justice to any of them?

If you identify with several of these symptoms; are dissatisfied with yourself or your relationships; you should consider seeking professional help. Arrange for a diagnostic evaluation with a licensed physician or psychologist experienced in treating co-dependency.

How Is Co-Dependency Treated?
Because co-dependency is usually rooted in a person's childhood, treatment often involves exploration into early childhood issues and their relationship to current destructive behavior patterns. Treatment includes education, experiential groups, and individual and group therapy through which co-dependents rediscover themselves and identify self-defeating behavior patterns. Treatment also focuses on helping patients getting in touch with feelings that have been buried during

childhood and on reconstructing family dynamics. The goal is to allow them to experience their full range of feelings again.

When Co-Dependency Hits Home

The first step in changing unhealthy behavior is to understand it. It is important for co-dependents and their family members to educate themselves about the course and cycle of addiction and how it extends into their relationships. Libraries, drug and alcohol abuse treatment centers and mental health centers often offer educational materials and programs to the public.

A lot of change and growth is necessary for the co-dependent and his or her family. Any caretaking behavior that allows or enables abuse to continue in the family needs to be recognized and stopped. The co-dependent must identify and embrace his or her feelings and needs. This may include learning to say "no," to be loving yet tough, and learning to be self-reliant. People find freedom, love, and serenity in their recovery. This is why many pregnant and parenting students are stuck in codependent behaviors and must be taken out of their chaotic home environment to develop healthier coping skills. They need the opportunity to live in a healthy and safe space like a residential academy for a few years.

Hope lies in learning more. The more you understand co-dependency the better you can cope with its effects. Reaching out for information and assistance can help someone live a healthier, more fulfilling life.

Teen Moms Anonymous

There is a new community-based support group called Teen Moms Anonymous.[2] Teen Moms Anonymous is a support group and recovery program for teen moms who are trauma survivors. Their mission is to help teen moms heal from violence and abuse. Participation is open to both teen girls ages fifteen to nineteen who are currently pregnant and parenting (with written consent from a parent or guardian) and adult women who were teen moms and still living with unresolved trauma.

The *Interpersonal Violence and Adolescent Pregnancy* report noted it is important for parents to heal from their own violent experiences in order to support the healthy emotional development of their children. When they don't heal, it can be a challenge for them to attach, offer consistently nurturing interactions, and attend to their child's needs and demands. Teen Moms Anonymous is a safe place in the community where teen moms can begin to heal. To learn more, visit their website—http://www.teenmomsA.org.

Co-Dependents Anonymous and Teen Moms Anonymous are two support group programs that can help teen moms heal from the violent experiences of the past. These are community-based support groups that offer a place for teen moms to heal at no cost.

> Teen Moms Anonymous is a support group and recovery program for teen moms who are trauma survivors. Participation is open to both teen girls ages fifteen to nineteen who are currently pregnant and parenting (with written consent from a parent or guardian) and adult women who were teen moms and are still living with unresolved trauma.
>
> —Teen Moms Anonymous

Summary

Support from the community matters. Support from the community matters because it takes a village to provide pregnant and parenting students the support they need. The community support is part of the village pregnant and parenting students need to graduate—community programs like teen parenting programs, parenting classes and faith-based programs. Support from the community programs played a major part in helping Xiomara, Toni, Quincy, Renee, and Kelly graduate. They helped them graduate. Other community-based support groups can also be a source of support for teen moms, like Co-Dependents Anonymous and Teen Moms Anonymous. Working together these community partners can not only help teen moms graduate, but they can also help them heal from the trauma of their past.

NOTES

1. Mental Health America, "Co-Dependency," https://www.mhanational.org/co-dependency. Accessed September 26, 2022.
2. Teen Moms Anonymous (https://teenmomsa.org).

CHAPTER 6

A Message to Teen Moms

The previous chapters provided information on how to help pregnant and parenting students graduated. Interwoven in that information was a reality-script version of what these students faced: being judged, being shamed, peer bullying, intimate partner emotional abuse, a lack of empathy and compassion from some peers and teachers.

Hopefully, you gleaned something from the experiences of graduates on all these matters as well as how support from home matters, support from school matters, and support from the community matters. This final chapter is specifically written to be a powerhouse encouragement tool to inspire pregnant and parenting students. In this chapter, graduates give hope to current pregnant and parenting students who are thinking of giving up and dropping out of high school. This chapter also includes an overview of the rights of pregnant and parenting students under Title IX, and what to do if they feel their school is discriminating against them.

Toni reminds current pregnant and parenting students that they can absolutely determine that success, excelling, and achievement is a choice that they can make and live out.

> Don't allow your circumstance to determine your outcome. Take into consideration your reality and move from there. Of course, your life has changed, but it's changed so what are you going to do now? What road are you going to take to ensure your success? Think about you and yourself five years from now. Think about what benefits you're going to have if you go ahead and attend school now. How much more beneficial that will be to you in the long run.
>
> Don't let a temporary feeling stop you from doing what you have to do. The thing about that same program, after I graduated, I came back and worked with them. So, I was working with girls who are currently

in school, and I loved it because I am them five years ago. I am exactly who you were.

I can identify and I can also tell you what blessings you will have going forward, given you take the time out. Take two years if you're going to a local school, take four years if you're going away to school, and I can only tell you how beneficial it is for you to go ahead and have that education.

> "Don't allow your circumstance to determine your outcome. Take into consideration your reality and move from there. Of course, your life has changed, but it's changed so what are you going to do now? What road are you going to take to ensure your success?"
>
> —Toni, a recent college graduate

Quincy wants you to know that college is possible for you. She wants you to know that there is something powerful about becoming a college student, especially as a teenage mother. "It means a lot. It just lets me know that I can do it, no matter who says I can't. It just lets me know that I can."

Xiomara is cheering on pregnant and parenting students. Cheering and waving flags of potential and possibilities.

Do not drop out of high school. It will be the worst mistake of your life. Keep pushing forward, even if you have to wake up and take it a day at a time. Sometimes it's hard to see. I know when I was in high school, I'm like, "Oh my goodness, I've had his baby."

You cannot see the finish line when you're in high school, but now I see the finish line, and it's like, nothing's better. If you have to wake up and just take it a day at a time, like, "I'm going to go to school today, but I don't know if I'm going tomorrow." Just take it a day at a time. Whatever you do, do not drop out of high school.

Alger says a green light means going forward is the right direction. There may be some detours and pauses, but success is the goal.

> "Just take it a day at a time. Whatever you do, do not drop out of high school."
>
> —Xiomara, college student

I would tell her to keep going and don't stop, no matter how hard it gets. It's all going to be worth it, and you never want to drop out and have to go back, because that's going to make it twice as hard. Just be an example for your child and just want to provide for them. Just keep going and pray.

Renee encourages pregnant and parenting students to hold tight to dreams. Dreams, even for teenage moms, do come true.

Keep your dream. Don't let the society down you because you're pregnant at a young age. You can make it. I made it. I graduated on time, and I'm in college. It's hard, but just think about it. It'll pay off in the long run. Your child will be happy, and you will be more happy about yourself because you didn't give up.

Renee, though cheering on these students, shares some tough love.

I see young teen mothers, and they're pregnant, and before they graduate, they got two kids, and I be one like, "You should have learned from the first one. Get on birth control." Having kids is not easy. If you're not financially stable, it's hard, especially when you're having problems at home. It's hard, you know if the father's not around, it's even harder. So, I'd tell them, "Just stick in school, use birth control, use a condom." Because you can't tell them not to have sex. They're going to have sex regardless. Just be smart about it. Finish school and go on to college. Don't drop out because it's going to be really hard on you then, with a child.

> "Keep your dream. Your child will be happy, and you will be more happy about yourself because you didn't give up."
>
> —Renee, college student

Hope springs eternal! That is what Laura wants pregnant and parenting students to remember.

> That she shouldn't drop out of high school and that there's still hope, a chance to do what she wants to do, and go ahead and get it over with, because there is so many people—people that don't even have children are trying to go back to school. They get to a certain age and they're like, "I want to go back to school," and that's the age they could have been done with school if you would just get it out of the way. Go ahead and just get it out of the way, and take care of it then, and you don't have to worry about it, once you're finally done, since you're done.
>
> But it's possible. You can still get through high school, get through college, if that's your choice, and make a decent living for yourself and your child. You'll provide them with someone to look up to, someone to inspire them in their choices later on in life.

Kelly implores students to remember that there is a whole world to be conquered; and pregnant and parentings students are well able to possess all that they see.

> I would tell her to stay in school. I would tell her there's so much more out there, not just for her, but there's so much out there in the world, so many different opportunities, so many different majors, so many different things that she can become.
>
> Don't view everything so negative. I feel like it's there's a positive to every situation, even if it's as simple as going to church and talking to somebody, or even just talking to somebody that you don't even really know.

> "So, I'd tell them, 'Just stick in school, use birth control, use a condom.' Because you can't tell them not to have sex. They're going to have sex regardless."
>
> —Renee, a college student

> "I want absolutely the best for my daughter. I've got to do the best I can do."
>
> —Kelly, college student

And this is one of my really big things. I always try to put the other person in my situation. For a teen mother who says she wants to go to college but is thinking about dropping out, I would put her child in that situation. How would you feel if your child had a baby young, and was thinking about dropping out of high school, or not even having a baby? How would you feel if your child were trying to drop out of college? Say that's like sixteen years from now. Say that the girl had her baby at sixteen, and that's sixteen years from now. Think about all the stuff that's going to happen in sixteen years from now. Think of all the technology, how fast the world is advancing.

I want absolutely the best for my daughter. I want her to be able to do whatever she wants to do in life, that's positive. I want her to graduate high school, good grades, college good grades, because I have good grades and I'm so driven and I'm so ambitious. I want to put that on her as well. I want her to be ambitious. I want her to be driven. I want her to be positive. I want her to be spiritual. I know if I want the very best for and I want to give her the best, then I've got to do the best I can do.

Finally, Theresa issues a challenge: know what is most beneficial for the ideal life for a parenting student and her child.

> The first thing is I would ask her a question. Who is it more beneficial to if you don't finish high school, or if you drop out? Who is it going to affect the most, you or your child? When I ask that question, I feel like her response would be, "My child" because she's a mother. Your child one day will grow up, go to school, possibly come see you and say, "Mom, I don't want to go to school." You will ask, "Why not?" And they'll say, "Because I just don't want to." What stage, what example have you set? With that being said, you have to pave the way for them, give them something to look forward to. It's beneficial. It's beneficial for you to at

least finish that level [high school], because if you don't, it just sets you back more and more and more.

I graduated in '98. If I wouldn't have graduated, I would have maybe graduated in '99 with a GED. The older you get, the more you don't want to go back, because it's embarrassing, that type of thing, and the less draw you have with a GED.

You have to go at night or whatever. It's just not convenient. I just feel like high school is there. Just tough it out, whatever you have to do to make it. There's programs out there, there's government assistance. Take advantage of it, use it as a steppingstone, and move on.

Perspective is key for pregnant and parenting students. Graduates who offered encouragement in this chapter and shared their stories in previous chapters know you have to keep a positive mindset. Pregnancy as a teenager is not the end of possibilities. You can still graduate and create the life you want for your family.

Knowing your rights under Title IX will also help you graduate. The OCR published the pamphlet *Supporting the Academic Success of Pregnant and Parenting Students Under Title IX of the Education Amendments of 1972* (2013) to make pregnant and parenting students aware of their rights. Make sure you are aware of your rights.

KNOW YOUR RIGHTS[1]

Pregnant or Parenting? Title IX Protects You from Discrimination at School

Title IX of the Education Amendments of 1972 ("Title IX"), 20 U.S.C. §1681 et seq., is a federal civil rights law that prohibits discrimination on the basis of sex—including pregnancy and parental status—in educational programs and activities. All public and private schools, school districts, colleges, and universities receiving any federal funds ("schools") must comply with Title IX.[2]

Some Things You Should Know about Your Rights

Classes and School Activities—Your School MUST:

- Allow you to continue participating in classes and extracurricular activities even though you are pregnant. This means that you can still participate in advanced placement and honors classes, school clubs, sports, honor societies, student leadership opportunities, and other activities, like after-school programs operated at the school.
- Allow you to choose whether you want to participate in special instructional programs or classes for pregnant students. You can participate if you want to, but your school cannot pressure you to do so. The alternative program must provide the same types of academic, extracurricular and enrichment opportunities as your school's regular program.
- Allow you to participate in classes and extracurricular activities even though you are pregnant and not require you to submit a doctor's note unless your school requires a doctor's note from all students who have a physical or emotional condition requiring treatment by a doctor. Your school also must not require a doctor's note from you after you have been hospitalized for childbirth unless it requires a doctor's note from all students who have been hospitalized for other conditions.
- Provide you with reasonable adjustments, like a larger desk, elevator access, or allowing you to make frequent trips to the restroom, when necessary because of your pregnancy.

Excused Absences and Medical Leave—Your School MUST:

- Excuse absences due to pregnancy or childbirth for as long as your doctor says it is necessary.
- Allow you to return to the same academic and extracurricular status as before your medical leave began, which should include giving you the opportunity to make up any work missed while you were out.

- Ensure that teachers understand the Title IX requirements related to excused absences/medical leave. Your teacher may not refuse to allow you to submit work after a deadline you missed because of pregnancy or childbirth. If your teacher's grading is based in part on class participation or attendance and you missed class because of pregnancy or childbirth, you should be allowed to make up the participation or attendance credits you didn't have the chance to earn.
- Provide pregnant students with the same special services it provides to students with temporary medical conditions. This includes *homebound instruction/at-home tutoring/independent study*.

Harassment—Your School MUST:

- Protect you from harassment based on sex, including harassment because of pregnancy or related conditions. Comments that could constitute prohibited harassment include making sexual comments or jokes about your pregnancy, calling you sexually charged names, spreading rumors about your sexual activity, and making sexual propositions or gestures, if the comments are sufficiently serious that it interferes with your ability to benefit from or participate in your school's program.

Policies and Procedures—Your School MUST:

- Have and distribute a policy against sex discrimination. It is recommended that the policy make clear that prohibited sex discrimination covers discrimination against pregnant and parenting students.
- Adopt and publish grievance procedures for students to file complaints of sex discrimination, including discrimination related to pregnancy or parental status.
- Identify at least one employee in the school or school district to carry out its responsibilities under Title IX (sometimes called a "Title IX Coordinator") and notify all students and employees of the name, title, and contact information of its Title IX Coordina-

tor. These responsibilities include overseeing complaints of discrimination against pregnant and parenting students.

Helpful Tips for Pregnant and Parenting Students

- Ask your school for help—meet with your school's Title IX Coordinator or counselor regarding what your school can do to support you in continuing your education.
- Keep notes about your pregnancy-related absences, any instances of harassment and your interactions with school officials about your pregnancy, and immediately report problems to your school's Title IX Coordinator, counselor, or other staff.
- If you feel your school is discriminating against you because you are pregnant or parenting, you may *file a complaint*:
  - Using your school's internal Title IX grievance procedures.
  - With the U.S. Department of Education, Office for Civil Rights (OCR), even if you have not filed a complaint with your school. If you file with OCR, make sure you do so within 180 days of when the discrimination took place.
  - In court, even if you have not filed a complaint with your school or with OCR.
- Contact OCR if you have any questions. [They] are [there] to help make sure all students, *including pregnant and parenting students*, have equal educational opportunities!

If you want to learn more about your rights, or if you believe that a school district, college, or university is violating federal law, you may contact the U.S. Department of Education, Office for Civil Rights, at (800) 421-3481 or ocr@ed.gov. If you wish to fill out a complaint form online, you may do so at: http://www.ed.gov/ocr/complaintintro.html.

In closing, as you strive to achieve your goals, to graduate from high school, go to college, create the life you want for you and your child(ren), here's a farewell bidding. A poem. Teachers should encourage their students to memorize this poem. It's a *reminder* to be resilient—to bounce back in the face of adversity. You may want to memorize it, too. On your journey to graduate from high school and/or college, when you're struggling or feel down and think about giving up, remember the words of your peers in the chapter and remember this poem: "Don't Quit."

Don't Quit

When things go wrong, as they sometimes will,
When the road you're trudging seems all uphill,
When the funds are low and the debts are high,
And you want to smile, but you have to sigh,
When care is pressing you down a bit,
Rest, if you must, but don't you quit.

Life is queer with its twists and turns,
As every one of us sometimes learns,
And many a failure turns about,
When he might have won had he stuck it out;
Don't give up though the pace seems slow—
You may succeed with another blow.

Often the goal is nearer than
It seems to a faint and faltering man,
Often the struggler has given up,
When he might have captured the victor's cup,
And he learned too late when the night slipped down,
How close he was to the golden crown.
Success is failure turned inside out—
The silver tint of the clouds of doubt,
And you never can tell how close you are,
It may be near when it seems so far,
So stick to the fight when you're hardest hi—
It's when things seem worst that you mustn't quit.

—Author Unknown

Take the ACEs Quiz—Prior to Your Eighteenth Birthday

1. Did a parent or other adult in the household often or very often . . . Swear at you, insult you, put you down, or humiliate you? or Act in a way that made you afraid that you might be physically hurt?
   No___ If Yes, enter 1 ___
2. Did a parent or other adult in the household often or very often . . . Push, grab, slap, or throw something at you? or Ever hit you so hard that you had marks or were injured?
   No___ If Yes, enter 1 ___
3. Did an adult or person at least five years older than you ever . . . Touch or fondle you or have you touch their body in a sexual way? or Attempt or actually have oral, anal, or vaginal intercourse with you?
   No___ If Yes, enter 1 ___
4. Did you often or very often feel that . . . No one in your family loved you or thought you were important or special? or Your family didn't look out for each other, feel close to each other, or support each other?
   No___ If Yes, enter 1 ___
5. Did you often or very often feel that . . . You didn't have enough to eat, had to wear dirty clothes, and had no one to protect you? or Your parents were too drunk or high to take care of you or take you to the doctor if you needed it?
   No___ If Yes, enter 1 ___
6. Were your parents ever separated or divorced?
   No___ If Yes, enter 1 ___
7. Was your mother or stepmother: Often or very often pushed, grabbed, slapped, or had something thrown at her? or Sometimes, often, or very often kicked, bitten, hit with a fist, or hit with something hard? or Ever repeatedly hit over at least a few minutes or threatened with a gun or knife?
   No___ If Yes, enter 1 ___
8. Did you live with anyone who was a problem drinker or alcoholic, or who used street drugs?
   No___ If Yes, enter 1 ___
9. Was a household member depressed or mentally ill, or did a household member attempt suicide?
   No___ If Yes, enter 1 ___
10. Did a household member go to prison?
    No___ If Yes, enter 1 ___

Now add up your "Yes" answers: _____ This is your ACE Score

NOTES

1. U.S. Department of Education, Office for Civil Rights, *Supporting the Academic Success of Pregnant and Parenting Students Under Title IX of the Education Amendments of 1972*, Washington, DC, 2013.

2. A school that is controlled by a religious organization is exempt from Title IX when the law's requirements would conflict with the organization's religious tenets.

Bibliography

10 Key Areas of Title IX, Education for Pregnant and Parenting Students. (n.d.). Retrieved from Title IX: http://titleix.info/10-Key-Areas-of-Title-IX/Education-for-Pregnant-and-Parenting-Students.aspx

Brene Brown on Empathy. (2013, December 10). Retrieved from YouTube: https://www.youtube.com/watch?v=1Evwgu369Jw

Brown, B. (2010, December 23). *The Power of Vulnerability.* Retrieved from TED: Ideas Worth Spreading: https://www.ted.com/talks/brene_brown_the_power_of_vulnerability

Brown, B. (2012). *Listening to Shame.* Retrieved from TED: Ideas Worth Spreading: https://www.ted.com/talks/brene_brown_listening_to_shame

CDC (Centers for Disease Control and Prevention). (2022, April 6). *Violence Prevention/Adverse Childhood Experiences/Fast Facts.* Retrieved from https://www.cdc.gov/violenceprevention/aces/fastfact.html

Charter for Compassion. (n.d.). *How to Show Empathy.* Retrieved from Charter for Compassion: https://charterforcompassion.org/discovering-empathy/how-to-show-empathy

Classroom Resources: Trauma Informed Strategies. (n.d.). Retrieved from Resilient Educator: https://resilienteducator.com/classroom-resources/trauma-informed-strategies/

Gonser, S. (2021, March 26). *5 Ways to Build Resilience in Students.* Retrieved from Educatopia: https://www.edutopia.org/article/5-ways-build-resilience-students

The Hechinger Report. (2018, January 22). "Fewer Teen Moms but Still a Dropout Puzzle for Schools." Retrieved from *U.S. News & World Report*: https://www.usnews.com/news/national-news/articles/2018-01-22/fewer-teenage-mothers-but-they-still-present-a-dropout-puzzle-for-schools

Hodgkinson, S., Beers, L., Southammakosane, C., & Lewin, A. (2014, January). Addressing the mental health needs of pregnant and parenting adolescents. *Pediatrics* 133(1):114–22. Retrieved from https://doi.org/10.1542/peds.2013-0927. Epub 2013, December 2. PMID: 24298010; PMCID: PMC3876179.

Leiderman, S., & Almo, C. (2001). *Interpersonal Violence and Adolescent Pregnancy: Prevalence and Implications for Practice and Policy.* Washington: Healthy Teen Network.

National Women's Law Center. (2017, January 5–19). *Let Her Learn: Stopping the School Pushout for Girls Who Are Pregnant or Parenting.* Retrieved from https://nwlc.org/wp-content/uploads/2017/04/Final_nwlc_Gates_PregParenting.pdf

National Women's Law Center. (2022). *A Call to Action to Support LGBTQI Pregnant, Expectant, and Parenting Students.* Retreived from https://nwlc.org/resource/a-call-to-action-to-support-lgbtqi-pregnant-expectant-and-parenting-students/

National Women's Law Center. (n.d.). Retrieved from https://nwlc.org/

North Carolina, Child Support, When Parent Is a Minor. (2022, February 14). Retrieved from Women'sLaw.org: https://www.womenslaw.org/laws/nc/child-support/when-parent-minor

Pregnancy Prevention: The Adverse Effects of Teen Pregnancy. (n.d.). Retrieved from Youth.gov: https://youth.gov/youth-topics/pregnancy-prevention/adverse-effects-teen-pregnancy#:~:text=For%20example%2C%20they%20are%20more%20likely%20to%3A%201,on%20publicly%20funded%20health%20care%3B%20More%20items...%20

Pregnant Scholar Profiles: Kamaria Downs. (2017, October 19). Retrieved from The Pregnant Scholar: https://thepregnantscholar.org/pregnant-scholar-profiles-kamaria-downs/

Reproductive Health: Teen Pregnancy. (2021, November 15). Retrieved from Centers for Disease Control and Prevention: https://www.cdc.gov/teenpregnancy/about/index.htm

Substance Abuse and Mental Health Services Administration (SAMHSA). (2014). SAMHSA's Concept of Trauma and Guidance for a Trauma-Informed Approach. Rockville, MD: SAMHSA's Trauma and Justice Strategic Initiative. Retrieved from https://ncsacw.acf.hhs.gov/userfiles/files/SAMHSA_Trauma.pdf

Supporting the Academic Success of Pregnant and Parenting Students Under Title IX of the Education Amendments of 1972. (2013). Retrieved from U.S. Department of Education, Office for Civil Rights: https://www2.ed.gov/about/offices/list/ocr/docs/pregnancy.html#_Toc15

Taylor, J. (2016). *Shame Resiliency Theory by Brene Brown.* Retrieved from Habits for Living Well: https://www.habitsforwellbeing.com/shame-resilience-theory/

TED: The Economics Daily. (2019, October 21). Retrieved from U.S. Bureau of Labor Statistics: https://www.bls.gov/opub/ted/2019/median-weekly-earnings-606-for-high-school-dropouts-1559-for-advanced-degree-holders.htm

This Day in History. (1972, June 23). Retrieved from history.com. https://www.history.com/this-day-in-history/title-ix-enacted

About the Author

Christine M. Stroble is an educator and researcher. She received her PhD in curriculum and instruction with an emphasis in urban education from the University of North Carolina, Charlotte. Her research focus area centers on improving education for teen moms and their children. She is the founder of Teen Moms Anonymous, a support group and recovery program for teen moms who are trauma survivors.

www.ingramcontent.com/pod-product-compliance
Lightning Source LLC
Chambersburg PA
CBHW020417230426
43663CB00007BA/1211